ROBERT GILL JR.

HAPPINESS POWER

How to Unleash Your Power and Live a More Joyful Life

TEACHINGPRESS

First published in the United States of America by

18 Bank Street, Suite 1
Summit, NJ 07901
www.teachingpress.com

First edition, 2021

Design by Formatted Books
Cover by Nathaniel Dasco

Publisher's Cataloging-in-Publication Data
(provided by Five Rainbows Cataloging Services)

Name: Gill, Robert Jr., author.
Title: Happiness Power: How to unleash your power and live a more joyful life / Robert Gill Jr.
Description: Summit, NJ: Teaching Press, 2021. | Also available in audiobook format.
Identifiers: LCCN 2020919813 (print) | ISBN 978-0-578-71832-3 (paperback) | ISBN 978-0-578-78044-3 (eBook)
Subjects: LCSH: Happiness. | Quality of life. | Well-being. | Mental health. | Self-actualization (Psychology) | BISAC: SELF HELP / Personal Growth / Happiness. | SELF-HELP / Emotions.
Classification: LCC BF575.H27 G55 2021 (print) | LCC BF575.H27 (eBook) | DDC 152.4/2--dc23.

Printed in the United States of America

DEDICATION

Dear reader when each of us turns to the dedication page, the first question our subconscious asks is, "Is the book dedicated to me?" So I know most likely you will be surprised when you learn that the answer to that question is a resounding, "*Yes!*" This book is dedicated exclusively to you and your future happiness, my special reader. Because you were my inspiration—without you, it would not have been written. I am incredibly grateful for your visit here today and your willingness to turn these pages. The truth be told, I believe you will enjoy it, learn from it, and be a better person when you are ready to put it back in its place on your shelf next to your bed. Now smile, as I want you to be happy as you go forward.

TABLE OF CONTENTS

THE HAPPINESS CHECKLISTS
(<u>Never</u> leave home without these.)

This checklist includes:

* ❖ The Happiness Advantage Checklist

The last thing we want is for you to miss out on your inner powers that happiness produces because you were not prepared.

To download your Happiness Checklists, visit:

<u>robertgilljr.com/check-list</u>

PREFACE

A young friend of the Nobel laureate, Bertrand Russell, once found the philosopher in a state of profound contemplation. "Why so meditative?" asked the young man.

"Because I've made an odd discovery," replied Russell. "Every time I talk to an intellectual, I feel quite certain that happiness is no longer a possibility. Yet when I talk with my gardener, I'm convinced of the opposite." What a profound sentiment—is happiness truly tied to intellect? Is ignorance, indeed, bliss? Bertrand Russell found himself in a bit of a predicament as he weighed that sentiment heavily, and who can blame him? Happiness is as complex and profound as humans themselves, and it can be hard to grapple with for many.

Happiness Power is a unique book that details how happiness's life-satisfying emotion provides significant benefits to those who experience it. It also offers those who seek happiness the latest methods and techniques to improve their outlook and gain the joy they are seeking. Happiness gives power to people who have achieved this state compared with those who exude pessimism and unhappiness. Most are unaware of the incredible power this book reveals. There is a deep connection between optimism and happiness because optimism reflects hope and faith, which help people to believe that this world is a good place.

Of the many emotions we experience, happiness seems to be the priority that people aspire to achieve. We can define happiness as a pleasant emotional state that provides joy, well-being, contentment, gratification, and satisfaction. Research on happiness has increased significantly since the 1960s. The studies have revealed that the realities of what contributes to happiness are often complex and highly individual.

Because happiness is what most of us are striving for, we should understand more about it. One thing is evident: Optimists are happier people. Optimism has many other benefits, too, which our book will examine in greater detail. For example, after conducting more than six hundred studies, Dr. Martin E.P. Seligman, Director of the Penn Positive Psychology Center, has found that being optimistic gets you the good stuff. By contrast, pessimistic people will often end precisely how you would predict them to—poorly. Winston Churchill described the relationship between an optimist and a pessimist aptly: "A pessimist sees the difficulty in every opportunity; an optimist sees the opportunity in every difficulty."

Tali Sharot, a London-based neurologist and researcher on optimism, recounts in her book *Optimism Bias: A Tour of the*

Irrationally Positive Brain that about 80 percent of the human population is inherently optimistic. Most just are not aware that we are. "The good thing is that when people realize that they have this hopeful outlook within them, it does not take a lot of work to develop their optimistic side."[1]

Having an optimistic approach to life is critical to attaining happiness. An optimist expects more positive things to happen than negative ones. Being optimistic impacts the level of our happiness as well as other aspects of our lives. Of course, happiness does not depend on an optimistic outlook. According to the 2017 "World Happiness Report," it is also dependent on factors such as care, freedom, generosity, honesty, health, income, and good governance. Nevertheless, optimism is a significant part of the formula.

Although it is hard to see the sunny side of the street, happy people have a way of turning the negativity that reaches them into positives more quickly than our unhappy friends. Now there is more good news for the cheery. A September 2019 study reported that optimistic people were more likely to live to be at least eighty-five years old. This finding was independent of other factors thought to influence life's length (such as socioeconomic status, health conditions, depression, social integration, and health behaviors), according to the researchers from Boston University

School of Medicine and the Harvard T.H. Chan School of Public Health.

Many unhappy people want to change their circumstances but do not feel that they can. In some instances, being unhappy or miserable is their way of life. That is because they often thrive on the sympathy from others. At the same time, unhappy people blame others for their situation. Sadly, they have no incentive to make life changes as they appear comfortable ruminating over their despair. Eduardo Andrade and Joel Cohen, in the *Journal of Consumer Research*, October 2007, evaluated why people enjoy horror movies. They concluded that some viewers are happy to be unhappy. Of course, unhappiness is not as simple as that, as we explain.

Christine Carter, a sociologist and happiness expert, sums up the benefits of optimism nicely in her articles. Compared with pessimistic people, optimists are more successful in school, at work, and in athletics. They are healthier, live longer, and are more satisfied with their marriages. They have better mental health as they are less anxious and less likely to suffer from depression.

In *Happiness Power*, we delve into the questions as to why happiness is so important. You might be curious about this yourself. Why is happiness considered a vital component of life, especially because there are many aspects to a fulfilling life? As you have read here so far, numerous scientific studies agree as to its importance. If not all, many indicate that satisfaction with life and well-being and meaning are integral parts of happiness.

Before we go too far, I want to admit that happiness is not necessarily the ultimate goal for everyone. It is important because it has wonderfully positive benefits. But we should examine the science for a better understanding. "Happiness science" is a new field of social science known as positive psychology. It is not the old-school "positive thinking" or self-help, but rather a new empirical research field. Positive psychology functions constructively to obtain more of what we want to make ourselves better, happier people.

This science was advanced after psychologist Martin Seligman developed the theory of learned helplessness early in his career. The approach details the response that follows when we believe our actions do not matter. It later led him to the idea that if we could learn to be helpless, we could also learn to be optimistic. This pioneering work is now known as learned optimism. It emphasizes the part that our cognitive processes play in maintaining happiness. Positive psychology was established in 1998 when Seligman made it his mission as president of the American Psychological Association to turn psychology's attention toward those elements of life that contribute to human flourishing. It does not deny the negative parts of life but argues for an in-depth exploration of the human experience's upper reaches.

With all of this in mind, can individuals learn to be happy? Numerous studies conclude with an ear-splitting "Yes!" Happiness is a learned emotion. The degree to which it is believed that you can increase happiness varies widely depending on which theory is being advanced. However, there are no credible theories that allow absolutely no room for individual happiness improvement. Experts agree that you can improve your happiness when you put in the effort to do so.

This book's purpose is threefold: 1) to make you aware of the extraordinary power of happiness and how it benefits a person; 2) to reveal how happiness gives special powers to those who achieve it, and 3) to explain how the power positively affects those around them as well as themselves. Finally, this book will investigate how making changes in one's outlook will improve happiness, along with all the powers that happiness confers.

Is happiness a choice? Is happiness power? How can you be happy? Are these questions that you ask yourself? If so, this book is the answer for you. Whether you are unhappy, purposeless, or just unsatisfied with where you are in the moment, you have hope. The good news about being unhappy is that things can only go up from here! But first, we should understand what makes us happy, as you will learn in our first chapter.

Now, smile! Let's get started!

Chapter 1

THE POWER OF HAPPINESS

"The 'We' are shaped by our thoughts; we become what we think. When the mind is pure, joy follows like a shadow that never leaves."

--Buddha

An ancient Middle Eastern morality tale describes what makes us happy.

Sukru came upon a sad-looking older man limping along the road to town.

"What's wrong?" Sukru asked.

The man held up a torn bag and cried out, "All of my worldly possessions barely fill this putrid, sorrowful bag."

"That is such a shame," replied Sukru.

Just as the pitiful man looked the other way, Sukru grabbed the torn sack from the man's trembling hands and ran off down the dirt road.

Now with everything lost, the gaunt old fellow fell to his knees with tears streaming down his cheeks. He was far more unhappy at that moment than ever before. But saddened still, he managed to climb to his feet and began his slow journey down the road.

However, in the meantime, Sukru had rushed around the bend in the road. He placed the sack in the middle, where the frail man would see it as he hobbled around the curve.

When the sorrowful old man saw his bag sitting in the road before him, he laughed with joy and shouted, "My bag! I surely thought I'd lost you!"

Watching through the bushes, Sukru chuckled to himself. "Well, that's one way to make a miserable old man happy!"

Happiness Power

Happiness does not depend on what we have; it depends on how we feel about what we have. We can be happy with less and miserable with more. Recent happiness studies have shown that money increases happiness when it takes people from a place with real threats (like poverty) to a reliably safe place. After that, money does not matter much. However, our story demonstrates how quickly melancholy can change to happiness with just a shift in perspective.

Happiness is indeed a powerful human emotion. Numerous studies have shown that happiness boosts motivation, creativity, and energy. It improves productivity. Research also indicates that happiness gives happy people greater power over their physical health. That is because feelings of positivity and fulfillment seem to benefit cardiovascular health, the immune system, inflammation levels, and blood pressure. It lowers the risk of cardiovascular disease and lengthens life expectancy. That power means that happy people get sick less often and experience fewer symptoms when they are sick. One reason that happy people have more influence over their health is that they exercise more frequently and eat more healthily. They are healthier all around and more likely to be healthy in the future.

Happiness reinforces the power of self-worth and confidence. Happy people view things differently than unhappy people. They are more positive and more focused on solutions. Happy people view their world in terms of gain rather than loss.

Happy people have immense power over misfortune. They have control over adversity, demonstrate strength over sickness, and offer advantages over life's reversals. This power provides them with greater success in business, social situations, and everyday life. It is an inspiring power to possess—inspiring because happiness is contagious. Happy people inspire those around them by elevating their mood. Yes, the power of happiness can seem magical.

There are more benefits to happiness. The power of happiness enables more success in marriages, added friendships, higher incomes, and better work performance. With more friends, happy people have a superior support system. They have an easier time navigating through life because their optimistic outlook eases pain, sadness, and grief. They smile more and engage in more in-depth and more meaningful conversations.

Happy people exert a positive power over others. It encourages others to seek happiness, as well. Happiness reinforces happiness because happy people are more helpful and more likely to volunteer, making them happier! Happy people donate more to charity. Giving has been proven to make one happier.

The Many Powers of Happiness. Happiness was a hot topic almost 2,500 years ago when the Greek philosopher Aristotle postulated that "Happiness is the meaning and purpose of life, the whole aim and the end of human existence." Happiness continues to be debated today. Since the 1990s, positive psychology has continued defining it. Happiness and all of its attendant powers are

4

more than just positive feelings. They are a state of well-being that provides significant strength to those who can experience it. Such powers include a vast array of physical and mental advantages. Accompanied with these powers are the feelings of well-being and a sense of contentment. If you could select one emotion to see you through a lifetime of trials and tribulations, happiness would be at the top of your list, as you will see.

Because happiness is such an important and sought-after human emotion, hundreds of academic studies support its many powers. (I list them here in short form, due to the length of the lists, to appreciate the powers of this seemingly magical emotion. Research is ongoing, and discoveries continue to be published.) We examine many of these powers in the chapters that follow.

The Fifty Powers of Happiness. The Fifty Powers of Happiness consists of physical, health, mental, workplace, and social powers. These are the most important of the identified powers that are gained by those who experience happiness:

Physical Powers

- Boosts motivation
- Induces more energy
- Improves productivity
- Improves physical fitness and provides stronger muscles

- Improves relaxation
- Enhances sleep

Health Powers

- Reduces frequency of sickness
- Reduces illness symptoms
- Reduces the risk of chronic disease
- Increases rate of recovery
- Improves the ability to endure pain when experiencing chronic illness
- Benefits cardiovascular health
- Strengthens the immune system
- Reduces inflammation levels
- Improves heart–lung function
- Increases flexibility
- Reduces stress levels
- Lowers blood pressure
- Lengthens life expectancy
- Reduces the risk of death by 18 percent

Mental Powers

- Broadens focus

- Improves memory
- Expands thinking
- Enhances creativity
- Nurtures greater generosity
- Fosters altruism
- Counters negative emotions
- Creates a stronger desire for community volunteerism
- Improves learning ability
- Improves self-worth
- Strengthens self-confidence
- Creates feelings of well-being
- Creates a more solution-based approach to problems
- Visualizes in terms of gains rather than loss
- Increases playfulness
- Increases interest in games and sports

Workplace Powers

- Results in greater success in business
- Obtains job interviews more frequently
- Receives promotions more frequently
- Results in better decision-making
- Enhances creative problem solving

- Improves individual and team productivity
- Provides better customer service satisfaction
- Achieves greater earning power

Social Powers

- Improves social standing and social situation
- Attracts friends
- Improves marriages
- Eases grief recovery
- Inspires happiness among others
- Increases desire to join social organizations

After absorbing this list's importance, very few people would say that they would not like to be happier. The feeling of happiness is a beautiful experience, emotionally and mentally. It is essential to a life of good health, social well-being, and your career. It makes sense that we would want to learn more about how to create greater happiness in our lives and others' lives. Let me show you how.

What Creates Happiness?

Do you remember this from school? The founding of the United States of America was in part based on happiness. The U.S. Declaration of Independence, written in 1776, asserts the right to "Life, Liberty and the pursuit of Happiness." But what precisely is happiness? How do the experts quantify it? Is there a more significant benefit to possessing a happier outlook over that of the more impassive realist?

Researchers think of happiness as having meaning and satisfaction in one's life. It is the ability to identify with positive emotions and rapidly recover from negative emotions while experiencing a sense of purpose. Happiness is not about material things, although they are always nice to have. It is also not the experience of eternal pleasure. It is a much more complex concept. Your ability to connect with others, to have meaningful relationships and a sense of community is what drives happiness.

Happiness promotes self-confidence in people, and self-confident people are the optimists in this world. Optimists surround themselves with positive people and face their fears and deal with them. Happiness flourishes with an optimistic person. But what about pessimistic people? Is happiness within their reach? It is time to provide common-sense advice on optimism.

Are You a Tigger or an Eeyore?

Gretchen Rubin, a happiness researcher and author of *The Happiness Project*, states that there are two types of people in this world: Tiggers and Eeyores. The Tiggers are endlessly optimistic, brimming with that positivity and bouncing with energy abounding. The Eeyores, on the other hand, are the opposite of their life's outlook. Their personalities lean toward pessimism.

Some of us are Tiggers, while others are Eeyores. If you are reading this book, I will hazard a guess that you probably identify more closely with Eeyore than Tigger between the two. It is okay if that is your default position, your natural disposition. The tendency to be less optimistic and focus on the negative is not something that will permanently keep you from happiness.

Research has shown that about 50 percent of our temperament has tendencies toward positivity or negativity. It is genetically predetermined, which means that you have little control over nearly half of your outlook. You cannot help that you see the glass as half-empty or half-full. It is just how your perception calibrates you. Those tendencies are a part of your genetic makeup, just as some people are more prone to be hot-tempered, while others may be more self-conscious.

The person with anger management issues needs to reorient their feelings to manage their life better. It is similar with individuals who lack self-confidence: They need to build their confidence to be more successful. In turn, natural pessimists will benefit by learning to think more positively, leading to more happiness power.

A twin study team, led by Lyubomirsky, Sheldon, and Schkade, studied two thousand twins from the Minnesota Twin Registry in 2005. They found that approximately 50 percent of life satisfaction was due to genetics, leaving 40 percent attributable to voluntary activities and 10 percent attributable to external events. They concluded that you have control over where you end up in life. As an example, you can choose to live a healthier life. You can select a career that you enjoy. Those are the kinds of factors that go into your life circumstances and, ultimately, happiness.

The research proves that happiness is within your control. A person can choose to control their thoughts and behaviors to create greater happiness. They can decide to make decisions that will bring them closer to the happiness powers over time. In summary, the research has shown that we could push ourselves into a state of happiness by better controlling our thoughts and feelings.

Even if you were born an Eeyore, you could learn to shift your thinking toward the Tigger outlook. You can modify the perspective through which you see the world. You can change the attitude that you have when confronted with unpleasantries. You can teach yourself to look on the bright side of things, and in doing so improve your happiness power.

Doesn't Money Bring Happiness?

For centuries, conventional thinking was that money bought happiness. After all, if you had money, you were not worried about meeting your needs. However, recent studies have determined that money does not influence happiness very much. In a recent study, the Nobel laureate psychologist and economist Daniel Kahneman demonstrated that money increases happiness until about $75,000 annually. After reaching that income level, emotional well-being no longer improves with income.

What is it that creates happiness (if it is not money)? If the ability to buy anything that you want on a whim is not happiness, then what is? Researchers have found that we are happier when we live fulfilling lives. Material wealth does not bring us fulfillment. What does, however, is the idea of "connection." Connection to people, that genuine connection that is fostered over time and endures through the years, brings us real, long-lasting pleasure. (I will address this point in Chapter 7.)

Dr. Robert Waldinger, Clinical Professor of Psychiatry at Harvard Medical School and the Harvard Study of Adult Development Director, spoke in a viral 2015 TED Talk that "good relationships keep us happier and healthier." The Harvard study is one of the world's most extensive adult life studies, starting in 1938 during the Great Depression. An essential finding of this study indicates that spending time with other people made study subjects happier on a day-to-day basis. For example, time with a partner or spouse minimized the mood dips that accompany aging's physical pains and illnesses.

Hedonism Leads to Happiness. Katharina Bernecker, a researcher in motivational psychology at the University of Zurich, found in a 2020 study that enjoying short-term, pleasurable activities that do not lead to long-term goals contributes as much to a happy life as self-control. This research from both the University of Zurich and Radboud University in the Netherlands suggests that people's capacity to experience pleasure or enjoyment contributes at least as much to a happy and satisfied life as successful self-control.

According to Bernecker, "Our research shows that both are important and can complement each other in achieving well-being and good health. It is important to find the right balance in everyday life." Bernecker argues for a greater acceptance of hedonism in psychology.

A Busy Mind Is a Happy Mind. A Harvard study revealed that stray thoughts and wandering minds are causally related to unhappiness. The study proved that those with continually wandering minds were less likely to be happy than those able to focus on the task. The study confirms what Buddhists have long taught: An unruly mind creates unhappiness and dysfunction.

Before we continue, it is essential to note that you do not have to be happy all the time to benefit from happiness. Happiness is not constant; it is cyclical. Happiness is broad and resilient, and the happiest people still experience negative feelings.

Neurochemicals of Happiness

Many of us agree that the human brain is a fantastic creation. From the day you are born, it functions around the clock. It only halts when you are about to take a test or attempt to speak to someone attractive. In Christopher Bergland's *The Athlete's Way: Sweat and the Biology of Bliss*, the premise is we retain the power to make ourselves happier through physical and lifestyle changes. Our body produces hundreds of neurochemicals. Scientists have identified a number of these chemicals, but only a small fraction of the amount produced. Happiness is little more than impulses in the brain, caused by chemicals known as neurotransmitters.

Several of them are directly responsible for happiness and optimism. These are dopamine, serotonin, and oxytocin. All three play a significant role in the body and create an individual with a more positive outlook. When you feel happy, it resonates throughout your whole body. Your entire body is under the influence of the hormones that surge throughout it.

A gene called monoamine oxidase (*MAOA*) affects these happiness chemicals' levels in the brain and is responsible for fluctuating moods in both men and women. Although it comes in two variants, we all contain this gene—a highly active and a less active type. This gene establishes how the brain processes dopamine and serotonin, chemicals responsible for making us smile.

According to a study from the University of South Florida, researchers have found a link between the *MAOA* gene and a woman's likeliness to report happiness. The researchers asked 350 men and women how happy they were and gave a saliva sample to test their DNA. The researchers found that 59 percent of the women had one copy of the less active gene, and a lucky 17 percent had two. They found that women with the less active type of gene were happier than others, and those with two copies of the "happy type of *MAOA* were happiest of all.

The study stopped short of determining that women are simply happier than men. That is because several studies have concluded the opposite is true. So, it is undecided. Happiness is subjective. For some, it is the fulfillment of creating. For others, it is joy or excitement. It is the culmination of all the good feelings, and it is something that people strive to reach.

Happiness Beyond Feeling Good

The power of happiness brings many more benefits than just feeling good. There is increasing evidence that happy people are healthier, more successful, and more socially engaged. Researchers Lyubomirsky, King, and Diener found that positive moods and emotions lead a happy person to behave in ways that help them construct their resources and capabilities, providing them with the ability to work toward their goals. Those qualities give them the power of success.

Researchers from the University of Texas Southwestern Medical Center found that serotonin, the happiness brain chemical, protects people against serious gut infections. Though serotonin was thought to be produced in the brain, about 90 percent of it is manufactured in the gastrointestinal tract.

Dr. Vanessa Sperandio, the study leader and a professor of microbiology and biochemistry, stated that "Gut infections occur when pathogenic bacteria, or the 'bad' bacteria, make their way into the gastrointestinal tract." Because gut bacteria are affected by their environment, the study's authors wondered if serotonin levels in the gut affected the pathogenic bacteria. When the cells were exposed to the serotonin-weakened bacteria, that bacteria were no longer able to inflict "infection-associated lesions." The additional serotonin caused the bacteria to lose its ability to produce an infection. The conclusion is that happy people have power over stomach issues—happy stomachs.

Does Happiness Come Before or After Success is Achieved?

Here is a "happy" surprise. There is growing evidence that happiness often comes before successful outcomes, rather than following it because of successful outcomes. In other words, conventional thought was that success makes people happy. Researchers Julia Boehm and Sonja Lyubomirsky at the University of California in Riverside had thought about this, too. Their study found evidence that it was happiness that led to success in many instances. That may be because researchers have found that happy workers have significant power over their less happy colleagues. They have found that happy people are more likely to obtain job interviews and show higher performance and productivity. As a result, they receive more positive evaluations and are better at handling managerial jobs. As the research implies, if positivity and success are linked, it becomes something that everyone wants to achieve.

Advantages of Happiness at Work

Some of the more essential benefits that happiness power provides you in the workplace include:

Better Decision-Making and Creative Problem Solving. A 2019 study by Brockis found that happiness at work provides benefits to those who experience it by the brain's changes and how it operates and thinks more efficiently. When you are happier, you avoid negative thoughts and issues that add stress to your life. Happiness allows you more room to think about how to deal with daily challenges positively.

Improved Individual and Team Productivity. In a 2015 study by Sgroi at the University of Warwick, happier employees were 12 percent more productive, and unhappy employees were 10 percent less productive.

Better Customer Service Satisfaction. A 2017 Gallup study showed that happier workers were more engaged. It resulted in better customer relationships, with a 20 percent sales increase.

More Earning Power. Another work-study conducted in 2016 by Tang found that life satisfaction feelings links to higher salaries; however, this varied between male and female employees. The study concluded that it was hard to determine whether having a higher salary led to greater life satisfaction because of having fewer financial stressors.

Our Power Over Ourselves

We are born with a desire to achieve happiness. Research suggests 50 percent of the way we filter the world is through genetics. However, 30–40 percent of our ability to make ourselves happy comes from our selection of activities—those things that we do within ourselves—our thoughts and behaviors.

We are continually working in a cycle of thoughts, feelings, and behaviors. It is a concept that heavily influences many psychotherapies, such as cognitive-behavioral therapy: You are creating your environment based on how you act. We all crave happiness. It is obtained by learning how to interact with ourselve and how to make better choices.

Consider this example for a moment. Imagine that you sat dow to take a test at school. You look down at the test paper and thin that it is going to be hard. You heard from people who took the tes earlier that it is incredibly tricky and tough to get through the whol thing. That thought makes you feel nervous. You are afraid that yo are not going to do well. Those nerves and feelings put you on hig alert, and your body naturally shifts into what is known as the figh or flight response. Your body thinks that there is a threat, and yo are, in a sense, if you consider getting a bad grade to be a danger t your well-being.

As you take the test, you are not in your best frame of mind. Yo are struggling to keep your mind clear, and then, when it matters the most, you choke. You do not get the questions right because yo are too nervous to answer them. As a result, you find that yo cannot focus effectively. When you get the score back a week later you discover that you did as poorly as you feared. When tha happens, you have now justified that you were right to be afraid You created a self-fulfilling prophecy!

The problem is that you have just effectively worried yourself into a trap. You have confirmed that worrying about your test was right, and next time, you will suffer even more. That is the power of this cycle, which applies to just about any similar situation. You can put it into the context of thinking about your positive emotions. You can choose to start with positive thoughts to create positive feelings, which, in turn, create positive behaviors. Think about the potential for a moment. If you need a positive boost, you can learn to talk to yourself more optimistically. When you do this enough, you repair many of your issues by substituting them with a positive approach. You can stop looking at the world like Eeyore and take the Tigger approach by shifting your thought perspective.

Maslow's Hierarchy of Needs and the Manifestation of Happiness

Maslow's hierarchy of needs is a theory in psychology proposed by Abraham Maslow in his 1943 paper "A Theory of Human Motivation" in *Psychological Review*. It is a theory in which you discover your needs and how those needs influence your happiness. You satisfy these needs sequentially. The approach comprises five tiers of achievements to reach your goal and source of happiness. As you achieve them, you gain more fulfillment.

Let's go over this hierarchy briefly to understand our needs and how they lead us to our happy place. The needs consist of two

categories: deficiency needs and growth needs. The first four need
on this list are the deficiency needs; caused by deprivation. (We
need it because we do not have enough of it.) We are motivated to
fulfill those needs to succeed, and the more deficient you are in
these needs, the more you are compelled to meet them. Growth
needs, on the other hand, are those on which you want to build
These are needs to help you feel fulfilled. They are the needs that
bring you happiness when you pursue them. (You do not pursue
these needs because you do not have enough. You seek them
because you want them. You want to grow. You want to be more
fulfilled.)

According to Maslow, you must satisfy your lower-tier needs
before you move up to the higher tiers. He created his hierarchy in
the form of a pyramid. The most basic needs are on the bottom, and
the rest follow upwards toward self-actualization at the peak.

Physiological Needs. The first category consists of
physiological needs. These are the needs that you must meet if you
want to survive. If you cannot reach them, the body does not
function properly, and, therefore, these are the most important
You cannot be happy if you deprive yourself of these needs. They
are food, water, shelter, warmth, sleep, clothing, sex, and other
physical needs. These needs will always come out ahead of the
others. If you have needs for anything else, these will come first.

Safety Needs. Next comes a need for safety and security. When you are physically satisfied, your next desire is for security. It comes in a variety of forms, for example, seeking financial security through employment. There are different approaches to satisfying the sense of security. As another example, you want to feel secure and in control of your surroundings and your life. It is where you start to see the influence of money diminish.

Love and Belonging Needs. After you meet safety needs, the need to belong follows. You seek out the feeling of belonging with those around you. You want to feel like no matter what you do, you connect to the people you love and care about. To accomplish this, you must be able to establish those bonds further. You are social by nature, and you naturally seek out some type of connection to those around you. The need to feel these connections to people motivates you to find others who are like-minded.

When you meet these needs, you are fostering your sense of friendship and intimacy. You are looking for affiliations, community, and love. You are looking for acceptance for who you are without any strings attached, and if you can get that, you are highly satisfied.

Esteem Needs. The fourth level on the hierarchy has two parts: esteem for oneself and esteem from others. Effectively, you need to provide yourself with the feeling of fulfillment by achievement. You need to feel like you are working toward mastering something that may be bigger than yourself. You need to feel like other people respect you as well. You seek prestige and status. You need to feel like other people respect you and your efforts.

Self-Actualization Needs. Finally, the last need, according to Maslow, is the need for self-actualization. It is the need to become the best that you can be. It is that desire to figure out what you can do to ensure that you are on the right track and better yourself. Self-actualization is effectively self-fulfillment. It is attempting to grow as a person, to accomplish everything that you can. It is where you start to get real, genuine happiness from what you are doing in life.

The Expansions to the Hierarchy of Needs

In the 1960s and 70s, Maslow began to add to his pyramid. He expanded the top half after studying what it was that self-actualizing people wanted. Maslow looked at what kept people motivated as they were achieving their self-actualization. He used that information as the basis of these last three premises of happiness.

The first premise is cognitive needs. It is the need to begin to understand and learn about the world. It is the need to explore, to find meaning and patterns in the environment around you. It is a need to have that innate understanding of the world.

Next comes the aesthetic need, the need for beauty. It is the appreciation that can come from looking at a beautiful painting or an expertly sculpted statue. This need to appreciate beauty in the world is a major one.

Finally, there is the need for transcendence. It is the understanding that we are motivated by values that are beyond ourselves. It is the idea to get beyond ourselves to experience being one with the world, seeking to experience kindness and altruism beyond ourselves. It is the need to be beyond ourselves and to reach out to everyone else around us.

Seligman's Elements of Happiness

Seligman began with a study of learned helplessness in dogs. Seligman noticed that some dogs would never actually quit when they were pursuing something. They would stubbornly stick right to it while other dogs would learn to become helpless. He drew inspiration from this, seeing parallels between people who grew depressed and helpless in their own lives.

This observation further inspired and motivated him. He realized a few key things: We can experience three different types of happiness that have separate meanings and contexts. We can experience:

- Pleasure and gratification
- Embodiment of strengths and virtues
- Meaning and purpose

His studies defined three types of lives that you can live: the pleasant life, the good life, and the meaningful life.

The Pleasant Life. The pleasant life understands emotions. It requires you to sit back and think about the past so that you can learn from it, thinking constructively. It also requires you to build optimism and look toward the future.

Studies have shown that happiness comes from developing a more positive outlook. It goes right back to the cycle of thoughts, feelings, and behaviors—the more positively you think, the better the results.

Positive emotions are associated with positive outcomes. While it may be easy to assume that happiness will create positive emotions, Seligman points out that positive emotions create happiness. With positive happiness follows.

The Good Life. According to Seligman, the good life builds on six virtues and twenty-four strengths. These counter many psychological disorders, and Seligman believes that they are the key to becoming a resilient individual. During a study with Dr. Christopher Petersen, an expert on hope and optimism, Seligman looked to create a classification system. They chose to use good character to measure efficacy because it repeatedly and strongly links to happiness.

They discovered that in nearly every culture, there are six core virtues. These six virtues became the stepping point for Seligman and his work. These six virtues are:

- Wisdom and knowledge
- Courage
- Love and humanity
- Justice
- Temperance
- Spirituality and transcendence

Alongside those values are several strengths, which are the methods used to achieve our virtues. They are moral traits that can be created, developed, and built over time. They are different from talents, which are typically inherited. The identified strengths are essential to living a good life. It is essential to utilize these signature strengths to bring about authentic happiness and gratification during this life. The good life is one of happiness, good relationships, and work.

The Meaningful Life. While researching happiness Seligman concluded that there are no shortcuts to happiness. To create positive emotion without moral integrity and character is an attempt to create something dishonest and inauthentic. A pleasant life may bring with it a more positive outlook, but it is not complete happiness. The good life is the same. It applies happiness through virtues to create a bigger picture, but there is still more. It becomes essential to work on meaning and flow to create a greater sense of happiness.

Happiness is a marathon. It is not something that you build or cultivate just because you have money or are attractive. It is not attained by having children or finding an ostensibly better-paying career. Happiness develops when you are working on something bigger than yourself. It is attained slowly, little by little, as you build yourself up. It develops as you develop your altruism. You find happiness by committing to people and positivity, by working to better yourself and find real meaning in your life.

Sounds excellent, daunting, and confusing all at once, right? It is, and that is part of the appeal. Happiness—real happiness—is not something that you can just buy or force. You must earn it. You must build it, fostering it bit by bit, step by step, until you know that you are in a position where you are making that progress that you were looking for.

Summary

In this chapter, we discovered the importance of happiness and found that it is a powerful emotion. The nation's founders thought the right to happiness is so vital that they memorialized it in the Declaration of Independence, along with "life" and "liberty." The emotion of happiness is so strong that it can impact your cardiovascular system and other vital body systems. We listed its fifty powers, which influence our physical, health, mental, workplace, and social being. We discussed a few of the hundreds of academic studies that support these powers.

We examined the age-old question, "Does money buy happiness?" The answer was surprising. The studies have found that we are happier when we live fulfilling lives. Material wealth does not bring us fulfillment. A Harvard study determined that good relationships keep us happier and healthier. A University of Zurich study found people's capacity to experience pleasure or enjoyment contributes at least as much to happiness.

We looked at the causes of happiness in the brain: the three happiness chemicals, namely dopamine, serotonin, and oxytocin. The "smile" gene known as *MAOA* regulates this. Martin Seligman's experiments showed that there are three types of happiness. He also hypothesized that there are three types of lives that you can live: the pleasant life, the good life, and the meaningful life.

We have some unanswered questions to pursue. If happiness is so powerful, how exactly does it affect our physical health? What do exercise and nutrition have to do with our happiness?

So, put on a big, happy smile and turn that page to continue our exciting adventure!

Chapter 2

HAPPINESS AND PHYSICAL HEALTH

"Our greatest happiness does not depend on the condition of life in which chance has placed us, but is always the result of a good conscience, good health, occupation, and freedom in all just pursuits."

-- Thomas Jefferson

During the COVID-19 pandemic, New York City's Lenox Hill Hospital played a famous Beatles song. "Here Comes the Sun" was heard over the loudspeaker every time a coronavirus patient was discharged or recovered enough to breathe without a ventilator's help. "The work is relentless," said pulmonologist Steven Feinsilver, M.D. "To hear this song on the loudspeaker is brilliant. It's just what people need, a reminder that patients are recovering. You feel good for a moment."[2]

One does not think about feeling good during a pandemic, just the opposite. While struggling to recover after a record-breaking health crisis, it may appear inappropriate to promote happiness.

Researchers have said that is not so. According to Yale psychology professor Laurie Santos, searching for and then finding happiness during difficult times matters. According to Dr. Santos, "Happiness gives us the resilience to get through. It is a challenging time because it's both a physical and mental health crisis. We need to focus on happiness more now, not less."

Amanda Griffiths, Lenox Hill's nurse manager, said, "The emotional lift provided by that Beatles song shouldn't be underestimated." Griffiths remembers that the song played almost twenty times in one day. She said, "Each repetition made me better. It was an overwhelming sense of 'wow, we're making a difference.' I got very teary-eyed."

Psychologist Maria Sirois, author of *A Short Course in Happiness After Loss*, adds, "The happiness that helps in great difficulty is realistic. It recognizes fears and anxieties. It looks for meaning. It nourishes and sustains us."[3]

Studies have confirmed that happiness influences health positively. The lead author of one study—Edward Diener, professor of social psychology at the University of Utah—listed several theories of how this might be. Happy people give themselves the power to choose healthy behaviors. They take better care of themselves through exercising, eating well, and getting adequate sleep. Research has provided evidence that happiness can positively affect the cardiovascular and immune systems, influence hormones and inflammation levels, and speed wound healing. Happiness is linked to longer telomeres, protein caps on the end of chromosomes that get shorter with age. In other words, happiness translates to health power.

Happiness and physical health have been linked for a long while, but happiness brings physical health. Or does physical health create that happiness for you? It is a question that is asked regularly, and the truth is, they go hand-in-hand. It works both ways, and ultimately, that is important to recognize. If you want to achieve happiness, you must be willing to put in the effort, to work on your physical health.

In this chapter, we examine what it takes to live a healthy life. We will go over both exercise and nutrition to see what you can do to help yourself be as happy as possible. This self-care is imperative if you want to ensure that you have a fit body and mind.

Exercise and Happiness

We know that our actions influence the happiness of our bodies For example, we might drink alcohol and feel happy in the short term, but we will not feel okay long term. Conversely, sometime things that might not be as enjoyable in the moment, such a exercise, will lead you to feel better in the long term.

It happens for one straightforward reason. Even if you dislike exercise or sports, there is a positive reaction in the body. The brain will release endorphins as you exercise, and those endorphin begin to reduce your stress levels. As the levels of cortisol and othe stress-related hormones drop, you begin to feel better abou yourself. You begin to feel more in tune with what you should be You ensure that your emotions and feelings are more along the lines of what they should be. That is all due to the positive effect of exercise.

Researchers have found that just twenty minutes of exercise i all it takes to elevate your mood. Those effects last for up to twelve hours at a time. That is not much time at all: Everyone has twenty minutes a day to give up in the name of self-improvement. It is a small amount of time to allot to boost our mood and work toward happiness.

While just twenty minutes will create the results you want to see, you should exercise more. Ideally, thirty to sixty minutes of exercise three to five times per week is the way to get the maximum benefits. Just taking a brisk walk will help, as long as you are consistent.

Now, you may hate exercise. Some people just are not very physical. However, the benefits are still there. First, movement tends to prepare your body for connection because your body responds when you move; your heart rate increases and your brain chemistry begins to change. The endorphins that fill your body when you exercise are the kind that also makes any socializing that much more pleasurable. The social pleasures that we often enjoy are much more potent when you get the endorphins pumping. That is why it can be such a great social activity to involve your friends and loved ones in exercise. It helps you feel like you belong. It makes that sense of belonging feel that much sweeter.

These same endorphins are known to reduce anxiety and pain. Creating those feel-good endorphins helps to defeat mental struggles, too. Some people have even shown marked improvement with their depression when they exercise.

Exercise also creates something known as myokines. Those myokines are linked to brain functions and are related to how your brain responds to stress and anxiety. Because of the resiliency that you gain with exercise, coping with stress is easier.

Happiness and confidence are also linked (as we have established). When you want to feel happier and live a more empowered life, you must be confident. Exercise can also boost confidence. When you work out, you are doing something that helps you feel accomplished. Exercise is frequently challenging because you are working your body. Because you have completed that challenge, you will naturally feel more confident.

Finally, research has shown that exercise is remarkably like meditation in its effect on the body. (Meditation is something that we will discuss in the next chapter.) It is the feeling that your mind is as clear and focused and in the moment. It boosts mood and aids in fending off depression and anxiety. Because exercising outdoors has a remarkably similar effect, it is highly beneficial both mentally and physically. It can help you open a state of awareness that you can use to reduce stress.

Tips on Exercising Regularly

We know that regular exercise benefits both the mind and body. That is because it not only builds muscle; it delivers the emotions of happiness and euphoria. To gain these benefits, you should try to exercise more often. That is where this section comes in. It is time to look at some tips that you can use that will incentivize you. These are natural methods to help acquire the exercise habit. Please consult your physician before beginning any exercise program.

The first step will always be the hardest. Think of Newton's first law of motion: the law of inertia. An object that is at rest will stay at rest. If you are currently living a sedentary life, you are at rest. You will resist the push to exercise. It will also take more effort to get you moving than it would have if you were already moving. It means that if you need help getting off the couch, it will always be more difficult.

Do not feel discouraged! You can get your body moving if you have the right plan of attack! Let's go over some of the best ways to get yourself moving regularly.

Think Small and Start Smaller. Before you begin thinking about overwhelming yourself, consider this: What if you under-promise? Do not begin with unrealistic goals; begin with mini-goals that you can quickly achieve. You need to be realistic, not only about your abilities but what you are comfortable completing. It is essential. If you want to succeed, you need to set yourself up for success. That means not actively sabotaging yourself with overly ambitious goals.

Start by thinking small. Begin with what is comfortable—it wi allow you to succeed in small steps. The purpose is to create a hab rather than a goal of strength and endurance. Once you establis the habit, you can then set challenging goals. For now, howeve even when you have a realistic idea of a starting point, scale tha back, too.

You may be asking yourself why you should even try if your go is to walk for twenty minutes in your neighborhood when that wi not get you fit very quickly. You want to make sure that you quickl attainable goals. You want to succeed at those first fitness goals t have that positive association when it comes time to challeng yourself.

Track and Plan Your Exercises. You should track not on your exercises but also plan them. You do not have to do anythin impressive. You just have to make sure that you are moving. Pla to get yourself moving for at least twenty minutes every day. Whe you can do that, you will start to see physical and feel ment benefits. It is the happiness creep.

Tracking your exercises has never been easier. There are s many different apps that can be downloaded right to your phone For the less tech-savvy, simply write down what you are doing an when you do it. By planning your exercise schedule and the monitoring it, you create an incentive.

Put the Gym Clothes Over the Alarm Clock. If getting moving in the morning is difficult, consider putting your gym clothes over your alarm clock. You may not want to get moving, but when your clothes are already in your hands, it will spur you on. Sometimes, just having to pick up those clothes is a great way to push yourself into moving forward.

Get an Accountability Buddy. Sometimes, having someone else who knows about your plans is enough to force you into continuing them. When you know that someone else will be asking you about your progress, you will feel additional pressure to succeed. No one likes to admit failure. Even better, if you find someone with whom you can exercise, you may feel like you need to be there out of obligation. After all, you may not want to admit failure, but you also do not want to be blamed for holding someone else back.

Get Rid of That All-or-Nothing Mindset. Finally, make sure that you ditch the all-or-nothing mindset. If you have planned to jog a mile on the treadmill, do some weights, and go out to play basketball with your friends, do not let the idea of doing all that hold you back. It may be that you realize that you got yourself in over your head, you realize that all of that exercise is an awful lot, and you do not want to commit two hours of your day. However, it is never all or nothing. You can always do just one part of that exercise schedule or choose to just go for a walk instead. Some exercise is always going to be better than no exercise.

Nutrition and Happiness

Just as exercise has beneficial effects on the mind and body, so does proper nutrition. A study from Australia recently found that eating fruit and vegetables helps you feel happier. The research suggests that people who add fruit and vegetables into their diets going from a minimal amount to eating eight portions daily showed a similar increase in happiness and satisfaction in life that unemployed people feel when they find a job. This improvement happens within two years of improving one's diet.

Of course, this builds healthy habits that will help your body. When you eat healthy food, you gain a variety of vitamins and minerals that maintain your health and good mood. It is the *happy diet*.

In a 2017 study published in *BMC Medicine*, Professor Felice Jacka of Deakin University in Australia detailed the positive effect of diet on happiness. Her study involved subjects with mood disorders; some were even on medication. Half the participants received counseling, while the other half received an altered diet. Those receiving an altered diet reported that they were significantly happier than those who just received counseling. The new diet included unprocessed whole foods, including more plant-based foods. It also included healthy proteins and fats that were associated with better mental health outcomes. The diets were high in fiber. Fiber is essential for nourishing good gut microbes. Dr. Deakin stated, "We increasingly understand that the gut is the driver of health, including mental health, so keeping fiber intake high through the consumption of plant foods is very important.

A German study reported similar outcomes. It demonstrated that consuming vegetables led to a higher level of happiness over time than sugar or unhealthy food induces. Of the 14 different food categories studied, consuming vegetables "contributed the largest share to eating happiness" measured over eight days. Sweets only provided "induced eating happiness" in comparison to an overall healthy diet.

A study conducted by researchers from the Department of Psychology from the University of Konstanz concluded with a final report stating the "findings support the notion that fruit and vegetable consumption has beneficial effects on different indicators of well-being, such as happiness or general life satisfaction, across a broad range of time-spans."

While researchers admit that they do not understand how these mechanics play out, they demonstrate that those consuming a diet high in vegetables reported a higher degree of happiness. Perhaps we eat junk food because it feels good. But the Australian study helps us realize that the more extended benefit of healthy foods is worth skipping the candy bar or ice cream.

Researchers believe that the benefits derive from the variety of pigments in vegetables. For example, carotenoids in carrots link to higher levels of happiness. Vitamin B12 is also in ample supply in fruit and vegetables, and B12 regulates serotonin, the mood regulating neurotransmitter in the brain.

Overall, what appears to be the best dietary approach is nourishment with as few processed ingredients as possible. You need to eat highly nourishing foods for your body if you want to be healthy, which is very intimidating. If you have lived your life only exposed to foods that are not inherently healthy, such as growing up on TV dinners, cereal, and bags of chips, you may find that eating fresh takes too much effort. However, better meal planning overcomes that issue.

Consider the Mediterranean diet if you need to look forward to something. This diet focuses heavily on the consumption of healthy whole foods that will keep you satisfied longer. You will focus on eating fruit and vegetables, with olive oil as the primary source of fat. You will also see moderate usage of cheese and red meats. Processed and fried foods do not exist on this diet. It is commonly associated with many health benefits, and it turns out that it is a great way to boost the mood.

Tips for Eating Healthily. The general takeaway from this chapter focuses on the foods you can consume that are healthy and nourish your body. Over time, you will come to prefer the taste of the healthier options presented to you. You will no longer have to eat junk food. Even if you have the option, the recommendation is that you make the shift to healthier whole foods. After all, how happy can your mind be if your body is undernourished?

Let's go over some easy ways to start filling your diet with healthier options for you to enjoy.

Enjoy Them in the Morning with Breakfast. First things first: When you start your day, begin it with fruit and vegetables. You can make a routine of enjoying fruit and vegetables at the first meal of the day. When you do so regularly, it will become a happy habit. There are so many vegetables that you can enjoy for breakfast. Toss some bell pepper and spinach or kale into scrambled eggs. Create a green smoothie. You could even opt for an unconventional salad for breakfast. Add berries to your yogurt and your oatmeal as another tasty option.

Make them Visible throughout Your Home. When you keep your fruit out and visible to everyone, where they are reachable, you are more likely to eat them. As a suggestion, displa your fruit and vegetables in a bowl on the table.

Keep Frozen Produce Available. Not all of your vegetable have to be fresh—frozen is a great substitute. You can reduce th hassle and opt to keep some frozen ones on hand. These are froze at the peak of ripeness, meaning that they are full of vitamins an minerals, and they benefit you in other ways as well. All you wil have to do is warm them up or add them to a casserole.

Make Vegetables the Star of Your Dish. We tend to worr about meat when it comes to planning our meals, but the bulk o your plate—the recommendation is half—should come from frui and vegetables. Planning your meal around vegetables is perhap one of the best things you can do to ensure that you made the righ choices.

Reach for Fruit Instead of a Sweet. When you crav sweets, consider adding fruit instead. You can choose to forego th treat, choose fruit in its place, or choose to combine them. Fo example, maybe you want ice cream. Instead of reaching for th caramel syrup, what if you added a handful of berries to it fo flavor? What if you took it a step further and pureed the berries int a fresh sauce? Reduce all the sugars. While ice cream is not the bes choice for the body, it is better to substitute the berry sauce for th caramel syrup.

Drink Your Fruit and Vegetables as a Smoothie. Finally, consider drinking those fruit and vegetables instead of eating them. There is no shortage of recipes online that will provide you with delicious, fresh smoothies. Smoothies create great options for you to hide those vegetables while enjoying the sweetness of the fruit.

Summary

Happiness has a significant influence on good health, just as good health influences happiness. A University of Utah study concluded that happy people give themselves the power to choose healthy behaviors. They take better care of themselves through exercise, better nutrition, and getting adequate sleep. Their research provided evidence that happiness can positively affect the cardiovascular and immune systems and even speeds wound healing. We learn that if you wish to achieve happiness, you should maintain good health.

Studies have found that just twenty minutes of exercise is all that it takes to elevate your mood. Those effects last for up to twelve hours at a time. Ideally, thirty to sixty minutes of exercise three to five times per week is the way to get the maximum benefits

Exercise boosts confidence. Happiness and confidence are linked, and thus exercising is another way to maintain happiness.

Start an exercise routine by thinking small and then working you way up. It may be challenging to get started, but once you do, you are building a habit. We provided many suggestions to maintain your exercise routine.

Happiness improves with the correct diet. The research suggests that people who add fruit and vegetables into their diets going from a minimal amount to eating eight portions a day showed a similar increase in happiness and satisfaction as unemployed people feel when they find a job. The best dietary approach is a nourishing one with as few processed ingredients as possible. We provided many suggestions to help improve your diet and keep you on the straight and narrow.

You might agree that all of that information is helpful, but how do you handle stress and negative emotions? What is mindfulness and how does that influence happiness? We will learn about that—and more—in the next chapter.

Think happy thoughts and turn the page so we can answer those questions!

Chapter 3

YOUR MENTAL HEALTH

"Happiness is like a butterfly; the more you chase it, the more it will elude you, but if you turn your attention to other things, it will come and sit softly on your shoulder."

-Henry David Thoreau

Here is a fantastic story that made it on the news around the world in April 2012. An eighty-year-old woman remained calm and seemingly stress-free as she crashed a small two-engine Cessna in Sturgeon Bay, Wisconsin. Before coming to an abrupt halt, the plane then skidded straight down the runway for more than a thousand feet. The report described the situation as she and her husband were from Florida, traveling to Wisconsin, and her husband suffered a fatal heart attack. Adding to the predicament, her husband's plane had only one operational engine and was running out of gas.

In a hard-to-believe coincidence, her son was in the control tower. He, too, was a pilot. He later reported that "Mom was calmer than everybody on the ground. She had it totally under control. The amazing thing is she landed that plane on one engine. I don't know if many trained pilots could do that. I already knew I lost my dad; didn't want to lose my mom. It could have been both at once."[4]

It can be challenging to cope with life's difficulties. When obstacles arise, you change your direction to reach your goal; you do not change your decision. It can be challenging to figure out what to do to provide yourself with the right attitude or the right kinds of actions to help you figure out what you need to do. It is challenging to cope with negativity or disappointment if you are in a position of not being resilient in the first place. It can be an issue for many of us. If you are stressed now, you probably will not deal with future stress well. Stress creates the opposite of happiness in our outlook. We all face stress in life—it is unavoidable.

Stress negatively impacts mental health. It leads to a reduction in the ability to maintain happiness. That is the subject of this chapter, as it is time to address the power that happiness has over mental health. Just as with diet and exercise, happiness influences mental health just as much as mental health influences happiness. The relationship between stress and happiness results in dealing with life's adversities with optimism and hope. A happy state is not constant. It fluctuates regularly. We must experience sadness to feel the power of happiness. You can deal with stress through an exercise in mindfulness while seeking the positive side of adverse events. This chapter will help you to do that.

Stress and Happiness

Stress is the body's reaction to physical or mental changes from your environment, body, and thoughts. It is a normal part of life. Though stress has a negative connotation, positive life changes, such as a promotion, a mortgage, or a child's birth, also cause stress.

All living organisms experience stress and react to it. There is a positive aspect of stress because it keeps living creatures alert and prepared to avoid danger. Stress has negative consequences when that organism experiences constant challenges with no relief. The result is that the organism builds up internal tension. The human body's autonomic nervous system has a response system that causes physiological changes to fight stressful situations. It is known as the fight or flight response. Such an extreme response can cause physical and emotional wear and tear on the body.

Based on research published in the *Journal of Happiness Studies*, people who choose to improve a specific skill experience stress. They are stressing themselves to learn. They have applied the pressure, and they are willing to invest what it takes to succeed. It is a beneficial kind of stress that helps them achieve their goal.

"No pain, no gain" applies to stress and happiness. When you want to increase happiness, you must stress yourself. You must push yourself toward the goal that you are pursuing. You make sure of your success by adding pressure.

Many tend to give up when goals are challenging, but that is when the true superstars shine. Think about how coal turns into a diamond under immense pressure. Similarly, stress converts into happiness if you know how to cope with it. It is where the skill of mindfulness is so helpful.

Dealing with Stress

Most stress is mild and not too upsetting. However, chronic stress links to physical and emotional problems, strained relationships, and severe mental health issues such as depression. Stress contributes to cardiovascular disease and exacerbates conditions like asthma or hypertension. Stress is inevitable in life, but it also must be well managed. You must manage your stress levels to ensure that they do not overwhelm you.

There are several ways to manage stress. Some of the most common include:

- Track your stressors and reactions.
- Make sure that you take the time to figure out why when you are stressed out.
- Pay attention to what is around you that stresses you out and fix the problem to ensure that your responses are under control.

Take a Walk. Remember, a quick walk is excellent for boosting your happiness and relieving stress. Walking produces endorphins, and as it does so, stress hormone levels dissipate.

Make Exercise a Priority. People who exercise often are also typically the least stressed out. They have the additional benefit of supporting their bodies and minds to make them more resistant to stress.

Say No. Stress can be the direct result of just being overwhelmed. When that happens, you have a few easy fixes. One is making sure that you say "no" when you cannot handle something. Doing so helps ensure that you are in control, and by maintaining that control, you can protect yourself.

Get a Good Night's Sleep. Your body is naturally less stressed when you are sleeping regularly and ensuring you are getting a good night's sleep.

Listen to Calm, Relaxing Music. Calming music can make your body and mind slow down and can aid in relaxation. It is an excellent way to deal with stressors.

Talk it Out with a Friend. Sometimes, the best approach to dealing with stress is letting it all out with someone you trust, such as friends or family members. These venting sessions can be great when it comes to releasing those pent-up feelings.

Talk Yourself Through It. When you talk yourself through the different stressors you are dealing with, you begin to develop resilience. It is imperative to handle your stress; this is a skill that everyone should have no matter what.

Laugh It Off. Laughter is the ideal medicine. If you laugh, the endorphins make you feel better. After a good laugh with someone, happiness shines through.

Drink Tea. Drinking tea can be an excellent way for you to cope with negative feelings. It may be a simple fix, but it can be quite relaxing to make a cup of tea and enjoy it.

Be Mindful. Finally, mindfulness matters immensely. If you want to minimize stress, you must be mindful. To be mindful, you must learn to live in the moment and let the moment you are in rule everything.

Of course, there are other options available. There are other ways to cope with stress. For example, you can choose to pursue a hobby or volunteer in the community. You can decide on an outside activity that will divert your mind from the current stress. In that way, you can work toward lessening stress levels and achieving that lifelong happiness that you seek.

Negative emotions are essential to survival. They are required to tell us what not to do. When we examine the purpose of negativity, we recognize it as an essential part of life. As a species, we evolved into a world in which everything seemingly wanted to kill us. We defended our way to the top to become the apex species, where negative emotions were advantageous. They helped us to be wary of the world around us. We exhibit fear, anger, anxiety, and other negative emotions to ensure our survival. For example, our anxiety serves an especially vital purpose: It keeps us alert when we are in a vulnerable position.

However, with the agricultural revolution, those emotions were not as vital. We no longer needed the constant vigilance previously required to ensure our safety. But the phantom need is still with us, and we still feel it. This feeling is similar to the phantom limb sensation, the sensory phenomenon that amputees experience when they feel that the absent limb is still intact. We still feel that inherited anxiety when we worry that something will not work out. We still get angry when we feel something threatens our beliefs.

As survival needs changed, happiness requirements also changed. With agricultural advancements came the creation of a new social system, which altered how happiness is perceived. Survival was no longer the determining factor of happiness– instead, fortune and luck replace it. Social status mattered. Financial security mattered. However, we no longer found our survival was dependent upon the tribe hunt. A new way to meet evolved, and we became more reliant on money and personal possessions.

However, material items do not create happiness. The technological revolution has pushed us further from the traditional method of acquiring happiness. As a result, those happiness levels have stagnated. With the COVID-19 pandemic rampant, the more we stay apart from our peers, and the more we are told not to interact with others and not be around other people, the worse moods become.

We know that happiness comes from interactions, and yet, the more technology we have, the more isolated we are from each other.

and the unhappier we become. Fewer social behaviors directly interfere with our ability to be happy. They prevent connections between each other. While technology can have an essential place in society, it tends to make us less happy. It adds stress to our lives, making it even harder to cope.

Handling Negative Emotions

Negative emotions can be incredibly detrimental to people. They hurt far more than they help. They are problematic for those who do not know how to manage their feelings. People who are positive and happy have an easier time handling emotions. Being able to manage emotions can make you happier. You will be able to slow down and address the source of those feelings.

Our negative emotions result from a myriad of sources. These are feelings that influence your thinking and can cause negative emotions. Those negative feelings are making things worse. These are emotions such as:

- Self-loathing—feeling wrong about negative feelings.
- Guilt—feeling wrong about good feelings.
- Self-righteousness—feeling good when you have bad feelings.

- Narcissism or ego—feeling good about good feelings.

These are all known as meta-feelings. They exist when w
attempt to avoid impulsive feelings, and they are responsible fo
much of the negativity in life. The Tiggers of the world see these a
things to overcome. However, the Eeyores of the world see thes
things as enemies, as villains that will keep them down even whe
they try their hardest to succeed. You need to choose which sid
you will take. Will you let these meta-feelings rule you, or will yo
take a stance against them to stop creating the narrative c
victimhood?

Now, let's take a look at some ways that you can manag
negative emotions.

Assign Meaning to Your Feelings. You can better contro
your feelings by assigning meaning to them. You need to recogniz
that feelings and actions are different. Remember that cycle tha
we discussed earlier. Your thoughts, feelings, and behaviors are al
interdependent. Because they exist independently, you contro
them individually. You can make the conscious choice to assign
meaning to your feelings to take control.

Choose How to Act. When you choose to assign meaning t
feelings, you will correct your behavior. You can choose how yo
will act. You can adopt a more positive attitude by choosing not t
follow the negativity you may feel. If you feel afraid, you can choos

to act anyway. If you are angry, you can choose not to lash out. If you are sad, you can force a smile. You do not have to let those irrational, emotional impulses control you.

Do Not Ignore or Bottle up Emotions. You cannot change emotions by ignoring them: Ignoring them will often make it worse. You will suffer the effects of the negative emotions the longer that you choose to ignore them. You need to acknowledge those emotions so that they can dissipate.

Even the more cynical, irrational emotions have a purpose. It is a message to you to understand their reasons. Take the time to analyze what your emotions are telling you. Are you angry because someone did something that hurt you? Do you feel frustrated by the behaviors of those around you? These reasons create bad behavior. If you can get to their root cause, you can more easily eliminate them.

Developing Self-Awareness

Internalizing negative emotions is harmful—it creates subconscious resentment. You need to identify those feelings. Are you angry? Why? Are you sad? Why? Do you feel irritated? There are reasons for all of these feelings, and the sooner you become

adept at figuring out what you are feeling, the sooner you ca
release yourself from their control.

This endeavor requires the skill of self-awareness. By workin
on that skill, you can identify why your emotions are influencin
you. Your self-awareness is something that you can improve ove
time. It is the key to becoming well-versed in understanding wh
you feel. It requires that you identify your behavior patterns t
recognize when you start to show signs of stress or anger. B
learning your patterns and recognizing what they feel like, you ca
begin to protect yourself. You learn to avoid falling for those sam
traps.

Question your emotions and their effects. After identifying you
emotion, it is time to determine what that emotion does to you. Ar
you the type of person who is continuously giving in to anger? Ar
you overwhelmed continuously or feeling like anything may set yo
off? Are you shy and refuse to interact with other people? What i
it that is going on with you that you need to understand better?

Mantras. A mantra comes from ancient religious Sanskrit. I
consists of words or utterances. The belief was that in repetitior
the sounds had magical or spiritual powers. When a mantr
utterances reaches the unconscious mind, the vibrations spread t
all aspects of your being. Nāda yoga incorporates such soun
vibrations in its mantras. However, the effect of mantras is not full

understood. Their sounds help heal physical imbalances, relax the mind, quiet the emotions, and open the heart. They stimulate, activate, motivate, and rejuvenate. They are an excellent solution for those seeking a respite from the negative emotions that strike us. Even if you do not believe in the mantra solution, it is a fun practice and does give you time to pause and clear your mind.

So, when hard times hit, take a comfortable seat, close your eyes, and repeat the familiar mantra, "This too shall pass." It is calming, reflective, and healing at the time you need it most. Force a smile as you repeat the words.

A simple mantra may not be the solution to minimize the effect of intense emotions. Grief, heartbreak, or severe anger can feel like they will go on forever. It is self-evident that feelings and emotions do not last. They will fade in time. It will help focus on the future, knowing that the current emotions are just a temporary phenomenon. But with time, these emotions do fade away.

Find the Source of Your Emotions. When you learn to understand the cause of your emotions, you can begin to repair them. That source is usually something with which you can easily interact once you identify it. By interacting, you can change your thought processes to a more positive outlook. That opens up the mind to receive happiness power.

Accept Your Emotions. To cope with those negativ emotions, you must accept them. They are what they are. You ca choose to respond to them differently. But presently, there is littl you can do to stop feeling sad after a family member has passe away. When something permanent happens and you react strongly you will have to accept those emotions. You will move past them With time, those negative emotions will fade, leaving room for th happiness you deserve.

Stray Thoughts, Wandering Minds, and Unhappiness Have you ever found yourself ready to do something, only to hav a stray thought cross your mind? Maybe you were sitting reading book when you remembered that someone's birthday is coming u or planning dinner you are hosting next week. You were sittin there, happily reading along, and suddenly, your mind i wandering away from your activity.

Wandering thoughts are detrimental to you. When you ar unable to focus, you are not going to be as happy. You will probabl discover how unhappy you are as you continuously fail to get o track. As was reported earlier, a study from Harvard Universit revealed that stray thoughts and wandering minds are causall related to unhappiness.

It is because the unruly mind, a mind that wanders abou without any control, creates dysfunction and unhappiness. I creates unrest. Your mind becomes a battleground for chaos, and focusing becomes difficult. The keys to happiness lie in taming that chaos to bring peace and quietness back to the mind. Effectively, what matters the most is being able to master your mind rather than trying to change the world around you. Remember, you can control your thoughts, and those thoughts that you can control are powerful. When you control your thoughts, you can ensure that you control everything that follows. When you can manage your thoughts, you feel happier.

Mindfulness

An element of the Buddhist tradition is a concept known as mindfulness, the psychological process of purposely bringing one's attention to experiences occurring in the present moment without judgment.[5] Mindfulness bases its form on Tibetan meditation. Buddhist traditions describe mindfulness as to how past, present, and future moments rise and cease as momentary impressions and mental phenomena. For thousands of years, religions have practiced mindfulness in various forms to promote well-being in an individual's life. Now science confirms these benefits.

In late 1970, Jon Kabat-Zinn, a microbiology professor teaching at the University of Massachusetts Medical Center, studied mindfulness meditation principles with his patients. His wor developed the Mindfulness-Based Stress Reduction (MBSR program. MBSR is now a course that advances secular, intensiv mindfulness training to assist people with stress, anxiety depression, and pain. His work also initiated a systematic set o research investigations in collaboration with one of the founders o affective neuroscience, Richard Davidson of the University o Wisconsin at Madison. (Kabat-Zinn's 1990 book *Full Catastroph Living* lists the MBSR program details.)

Mindfulness is a potent state, directly linked to happiness, a feelings of well-being increase when people tap into them Mindfulness is a state of being in the moment. It is the ultimat state of being connected to what you are doing by focusing th mind. We already use mindfulness without really thinking about i Think of the state that you get into when you are watching compelling show on television. You are fixated, drawn to th characters, and the only thing you focus on is what is on the screen That is a state of mindfulness. You can mindfully do just abou anything, from hiking to eating and even cleaning. The idea is t focus your mind.

If you had to define it, mindfulness is a state of purposefull focusing all of your attention on the present moment, acceptin what is happening around you without judgment.[6] It is acceptin anything that is happening as valid and trying not to fight it. That acceptance, that simple surrender to what is happening around you, is the key to reducing your stress. When you stop trying to change things that surround you because you acknowledge the futility of attempting to do so, you can let go of a whole level of stress. You can forego the feelings of anxiety that will otherwise threaten to control you. You just accept the feeling and move on without judgment. To be mindful creates physical and emotional benefits. When you can master this process, you will find that your general physical and mental well-being will improve.

One of the most pertinent benefits and uses of mindfulness is that it is featured heavily in many psychotherapy forms. Using it regularly ensures that you can better cope with your emotions and problems that you may otherwise face. Cognitive-behavioral therapy focuses on mindfulness as a way to work through the emotional turmoil that you may face so that you will be able to cope in the future. By learning mindfulness and meditation, you develop an option that enables you to sit back, accept what is happening around you, and prevent yourself from responding in ways that would otherwise be unproductive.

How to Be Mindful

If you want to be mindful, there are effortless ways that you can develop the practice. Mindfulness becomes a skill that you can take with you anywhere that you go. It becomes an instant defense against feeling stressed or overwhelmed. It is something that you can rely upon if you ever find yourself needing to keep focused. Let us examine what it takes to master mindfulness.

Practice during Routine Activities. Mindfulness is something that you can easily practice. One of the best times to begin training is when you start practicing routine activities. The best way to be mindful when you need to is to be mindful when you do not. It assists you to get used to the sensation and what you will need to get into it. The best way to begin is to be mindful when doing routine activities such as brushing your teeth or driving. When you do this, focusing on all of the sensations that go along with them, you learn acceptance. You learn to accept what is happening with your body as it happens so that when you have those strong emotions, you can let them wash over you without responding to them.

Practice When You First Wake Up. Another opportunity for working on mindfulness is to practice it as soon as you wake up. When you spend your first moments of the day mindfully, you can help start your day off on the right foot. If you find that doing so first thing in the morning is too much for you and that you start dozing off during your practice, have your coffee first and then use mindfulness before looking at your phone.

Let Your Mind Wander. Your mind wanders naturally. While letting stray thoughts control you is often problematic; having a busy brain is an asset. When you want to think mindfully, all you have to do is gently return your thoughts to the topic you focused on before your mind goes too astray.

Keep It Short. When you are first practicing mindfulness, keep the session short. Short sessions several times per day are better than just one long session. You want to keep this process positive and beneficial. You want to make sure that you are happy with the progress that you are making. Most of all, you want to ensure that mindfulness does not become a chore. Choose short periods for a minute or two to practice mindfulness in the moment now and then.

Wait Mindfully. A reasonable time to practice a spurt of mindfulness is when you are waiting. If you are waiting in line to get some food or check out at the store, simply let yourself focus on the sensations. Feel the moment and allow yourself to focus on the flow of it. It is an excellent short reminder of mindfulness that can help you.

Pick a Mantra or Other Prompt to Remind Yourself to Be Mindful. At times, we need a reminder of what we need in life. It could be a word or phrase for mindfulness, or it could be something that you do. Maybe drinking your coffee becomes paired with your need for mindfulness. Every time that you find yourself drinking a coffee, you can practice for a moment or two. This habit helps you to build mindfulness into your routine. It aids you in learning what it is that you need.

Learn to Meditate. One last thing that you can do to cultivate your mindfulness is to learn to meditate. Meditation is helpful, and the sooner you can master it, the sooner you can become capable of entering that state of mindfulness.

Meditation is the act of triggering that mindfulness. It is practicing the mental language, the functionality of being mindful. It can be awkward at first, but you can train your brain to be more efficient in avoiding distractions with practice.

How to Meditate. Meditation is not about understanding how to empty your mind or stop your thoughts. When we meditate mindfully, we learn to focus without judgment. Mindfulness meditation is the most common type of meditation practiced in the West, perhaps the easiest for beginners.

Practicing mindfulness for meditation begins with following these steps:

1. Set aside the time to do so.
2. Sit in a quiet place.
3. Observe the moment that you are currently in without judgment or attempting to change it.
4. Push away your judgments without letting them influence your thoughts or your actions.
5. When your mind wanders, return it to the present moment without judgment or admonishment.

Be kind when you notice that you are wandering, and make sure that you recognize that you owe yourself gentleness and grace.

When you can follow those five steps, you will create that mindful state to help you decide that it is time to meditate. We are going to go over a special breathing meditation that will help you to sit and focus. Breathing may not seem like much. After all, it is something that you continuously do as long as you are living. However, breathing is also immensely powerful. It can influence how your body and mind function because you can calm yourself using breathing and the natural reflexes. Being able to breathe mindfully, then, becomes something that can influence your entire being.

Meditation will have you focus on your breathing to focus calm yourself and gain the benefits that come with it.

Step 1: Sit comfortably. Start by finding somewhere comfortable to sit. It should be somewhere that makes you feel grounded. You should feel like you can sit firmly and stably to focus.

Step 2: Pay attention to your legs. What you do with them is up to personal preference. Sitting with your legs crossed is fine. However, you can also sit with your feet planted firmly on the floor while sitting on a chair or another raised surface. Just do what feels the most comfortable.

Step 3: Keep the correct upper body posture. Next comes the focus on your posture. You want to sit up straight without being stiff. You should allow for the natural curvature of your spine to be in place to be as comfortable as possible.

Step 4: Pay attention to your arms. You should make sure that also you keep your arms comfortable. They should be parallel to the rest of your upper body. Your palms should be resting naturally either on the chair you sit on or on your legs. The important part is staying comfortable.

Step 5: Control your gaze. Allow your chin to relax and drop letting your gaze naturally rest in front of you at a slightly downward angle. Meditation is accomplished with your eyes open or closed. Many beginners find it easiest with closed eyes.

Step 6: Focus on your breathing. Shift your attention to your breathing. You should concentrate on the feeling of the air coming through your mouth or nose and how it makes your chest rise and fall. Pay attention to how your stomach moves as well the sensation of the breath exiting your nose. Some people like to slow their breathing down during this time with a pattern of taking four seconds, breathing in, and four seconds breathing out. If you find that your mind starts to wander, just redirect it to return it to your breathing.

Step 7: Remember compassion for yourself. Be kind to yourself during this time. It is usual for your mind to wander. It will do so out of habit if you are not focusing on it. When this happens, the solution is to redirect your mind back to what you are doing and focus. You want to be kind to yourself. You want to make sure that you keep a positive association with the meditation.

Step 8: Release the mindfulness. Finally, when complete, all you have to do is shift your attention. Instead of paying attention to your mind and your breathing, look around your environment. Focus on how you feel at the moment. How are you doing emotionally? Mentally? Physically? You have just spent a significant amount of time meditating, which is a great thing. Reflect upon that and enjoy the benefits.

Summary

We learned that stress leads to a reduction in our ability t maintain happiness. While there is a positive aspect to stress, as keeps living creatures alert and prepared to avoid danger, negativ emotions can be detrimental, as they hurt far more than they hel Those negative feelings, known as *meta-feelings*, can make you fe unhappy. You can control those feelings by assigning meaning t them.

An excellent way to reduce negative feelings is wit introspection through self-awareness. Once you identify you emotion, you can more easily determine what that emotion does t you. Consider using a mantra for this purpose, such as repeating "This too shall pass," to yourself. It will help you focus.

Try to prevent wandering thoughts. The inability to focus lead to unhappiness. An element of the Buddhist tradition is a concep known as *mindfulness*. For thousands of years, mindfulness i various forms has been practiced to cultivate well-being in a individual's life. Mindfulness is something that you can quickl develop.

Meditation triggers mindfulness. When we meditate mindfully we learn to focus without judgment. Mindfulness meditation is th most common type of meditation practiced in the West an perhaps the easiest to begin. These are essential lessons on the path to happiness.

We have yet to mention gratitude. How does that figure in our happiness? How does it eliminate guilt, which interferes with our happiness? The answers to these questions and many others are in the very compelling next chapter.

Let's discover the answers together.

Chapter 4

THE POWER OF GRATITUDE

"Until you learn to be grateful for the things you have, you will not receive the things you want."

--John Kralik

A blind boy set a sign next to his feet that read, "I am blind, can you help me?" He sat on the building's steps holding out his hat and hope.

The hat only held a few coins provided by strangers as they hurried past the boy. A man soon came by and took all the change from his pocket and dropped it in the boy's hat. Then, without the boy's knowledge, he picked up the sign, changed the words, and carefully returned it to its position next to the boy's feet.

To the boy's surprise, the hat rapidly filled up. There were so many people giving now.

Later in the day, the man returned. The boy recognized the sound of his familiar footsteps and asked, "Are you the man with all the change? Did you also change my sign this morning? Please what did you write?"

The generous stranger replied, "I wrote only truth. I rewrote what you wrote but only in a more detailed way. The sign now read 'Today is a beautiful day, but I cannot see it.'

Both signs were undoubtedly correct. However, the first sign stated that the boy was blind, while the second sign conveyed to everyone walking by how grateful they should be to see.

Gratitude is incredibly powerful if you open your heart up to it. It can improve your happiness significantly just by inviting it into your life. It is also a way that you can spread happiness. When you are grateful, you are far more likely to achieve happiness by showing gratitude to other people. You will have better relationships, feel more significant, and focus on the positive. Researchers are looking at measuring and predicting positive emotions to share the critical circumstances responsible and the skills to practice to be happier. Many excellent studies about gratitude's relationship to happiness are available. We will introduce some important ones to you in this chapter.

Robert C. Roberts's 2004 book *The Blessings of Gratitude: A Conceptual Analysis* postulated that gratitude promotes human well-being by reducing dispositions to resentment, regret, and envy. Frederickson's 2004 work on positive emotions revealed that gratitude often leads to giving back to others, creating more opportunities for positive emotions and experiences.

In a 2018 study, "Gratitude Predicts Hope and Happiness: A Two-Study Assessment of Traits and States," Dr. Charlotte van Oyen Witvliet and her research team studied how gratitude predicts hope and happiness. Positive psychology research has identified that gratitude is associated with happiness. Their theory of gratitude was inspired by Robert C. Roberts's book on the subject. They found that "gratitude is about givers, gifts, recipients, and the attitudes of givers and recipients toward one another." Gratitude, compared with joy and hope, is a much deeper emotion, whereas joy results from a behavior or action, and hope is a thought of a future action for good. Gratitude magnifies whether the conferred benefit is unexpected or whether the giver is of a higher social status than the receiver.

In this chapter, we will examine the power of gratitude. We will observe what goes into this emotion and how you can use it successfully in your own life. We will study what it will take for you to better connect with other people to bond better, and we will look at the benefits of being a more grateful person.

What is Gratitude?

As we will discuss in Chapter 7, we need people. We are social animals and, as such, thrive on relationships with others. We see that connection and feeling of belonging, as we saw in examining Maslow's *Hierarchy of Needs*. Gratitude is how we establish that connection.

Research has shown that people who live more grateful lives are happier, more satisfied, and less vulnerable to discomfort. The benefits of gratitude are numerous. Before we begin to address why gratitude and happiness go hand in hand, let's take some time to address what gratitude is.

Gratitude is an emotion that has been a major focus in positive psychology research. It is quite similar to appreciation but not quite the same. It has a neurological basis in the benefits that it provides. By expressing gratitude, you engage your brain in ways that are beneficial, influential, and help you succeed. It is something that many people understand but struggle to define. It is more than just saying "thank you" after receiving a gift or being helped. It is a physiological state that offers incredible benefits. It is more than just feeling thankful. It is a more profound appreciation that lasts longer and endures through time.

Harvard Medical School created one of the better descriptions. It defines gratitude as "a thankful appreciation for what was received, acknowledging the goodness in one's life." It connects people on a grander scale than just in the moment. It is a recognition of the fact that we can provide value and meaning that is appreciated. It is seeing that someone has helped you somehow and understanding that they have put in their effort to do so. They have given up their time and potentially their resources to you, and you respect it.

According to Dr. Robert Emmons, gratitude appears in two phases. The first stage is acknowledging what has happened. To be grateful, you acknowledge that your life is currently full of goodness, which you must acknowledge and affirm. Life is good, even if it is full of challenges that can make things difficult. Even when you struggle, there is still a goodness that must be acknowledged. When you can do that, seeing the bigger picture and the brighter side of things, you begin to do better. Your gratitude begins to bring you happiness more profoundly than you thought was possible.

Recognize that goodness comes from outside yourself. Gratitude comes from looking to the goodness that is external to you. You can be grateful to animals that provide nourishment. You can be grateful to your dog for being your best friend when you need him the most. You can be grateful to your family and friend and even to strangers. However, gratitude is not inward. Gratitud is not something that you direct toward yourself.

In the second stage of gratitude, you recognize that goodnes comes from outside of yourself. It is the stage where you realize tha your happiness comes from your spouse for being there for you; i comes from your parents, who have dedicated their lives to raisin you; it comes from the teachers and mentors along the way, wh have helped you to become the person that you are today. You ca recognize that these people have sacrificed for your betterment The way that they were able to better you becomes their gift to yo for which you can give thanks.

Gratitude is inherently selfless. It is unconditional and show internal appreciation toward other people. Doing so can influenc two critical processes in your life, namely catharsis and reciprocit Both of these responses are directly related to your happiness.

Let's look first at *catharsis*. Psychology defines it as a release o strong emotions. It may happen after a trauma or through cryin to release your emotions. It can also play a role in gratitude Consider a situation in which you have failed to meet a deadline Perhaps you needed to complete a report for work and you fel behind. You feel guilt. You are concerned that you have failed anc that your failure will hurt those around you. Instead of expressin guilt, you can express gratitude. By telling them that you appreciate that you have done something that makes life harder for them, it can help offset their disappointment. Consider the difference between apologizing to someone for being late, focusing on the negative, versus thanking the other person for waiting for you. The latter is being grateful to them for their patience. This shift to focus on the good instead of the bad is a great start to ensuring that you can positively express that positivity. Gratitude serves as the sense of catharsis in this situation instead of guilt.

You can also consider reciprocity, a social psychology concept that shows an exchange between two people. In gratitude, the exchange is through positive emotions. When someone acts in gratitude, you motivate the recipient to be grateful. Think of this as the "pay it forward." One person pays for the person behind them, and the person behind them, moved by the gratitude, pays for the next person and creates a chain of events.

Gratitude and Happiness

We know that gratitude is contagious, and we know that it can influence other people's well-being. Now it is time to examine why. Gratitude links to positive benefits such as happiness, positivity, better health, and coping with stress and adversity. It builds good relationships. These outcomes are because gratitude brings several key benefits.

Gratitude Promotes Focusing on Positive Life Experiences. When we are busy, it can be easy to forget to stop and savor the moment. Think about the cliché of parents stopped by older people smiling wistfully and saying, "Enjoy it while it lasts!" It happens for a reason. We tend not to appreciate what we have until it is gone. Often, we find it easier to concentrate on the negative in life. We focus on what goes wrong more than what goes right, and there is a biological purpose for that: It keeps us alive. However, it also keeps us unhappy at times. Happiness comes from that state of gratitude, from recognizing that what we have is better than we probably thought. Even when it seems like your luck has left you, you can find positivity if you look for it, and the sooner you practice it, the better you will feel. Gratitude is the key to doing exactly that. With gratitude, you will see how you can better focus on what you need to do. You will discover how you can pay attention to what matters the most in life.

Gratitude Bolsters Self-Worth and Self-Esteem. Gratitude helps you see yourself as better than you may have before. With gratitude, you recognize that you have accomplished more than that for which you give yourself credit. You can see that other people have stopped to help you. When you are grateful, you pay attention to the people who have helped influence you. You see the ways that others are kind to you. You feel more positive because you see that others care about you. You see that you are worth focusing on and that you are deserving. Seeing what other people see in you and that other people are investing in you helps you better focus on yourself.

Gratitude Helps to Cope with Stress and Trauma. Gratitude can help people cope with stress and trauma. When it comes to suffering through these circumstances, gratitude can help you redirect your focus. When you shift your focus, you can also better yourself. Grateful people can interpret those negative emotions in a positive light. It is precisely why, in the face of tragedy and adversity, you see people who can focus on the positive recovering sooner.

Gratitude Encourages Moral Behaviors. Gratitude and morality are linked. In particular, gratitude tends to encourage altruistic behavior. When you are grateful, you usually see that the good in life is external, focusing on that point. You pay attention to what you are doing and how you can influence those around you. As a result, you pick up on those better, more positive behaviors. Gratitude encourages people to be more helpful to others and less concerned with physical, material goods. Grateful people can

recognize that what they have is not permanent and know they hav
what they have because others have contributed.

Because of reciprocity, if you do something kind for someone
they are likely to want to repay that act later in their gratitude. I
doing this, you can create and foster gratitude, not just in yourse
but also in everyone else.

Gratitude Journals

Social bonds are built and strengthened through gratitude. A
further evidence for that, in Arianna Huffington's book *Thrive*, sh
reports on a study by researchers from the University of Minnesot
and the University of Florida. They had participants record a list o
positive events at the end of the day and the reasons that mad
them happy. The researchers found that this activity lowered thei
self-reported stress levels and gave them a greater sense of calm. A
gratitude journal is a diary of things for which one is thankful
Gratitude journals are used by those who wish to concentrate o
the positive things in their lives. People who use them show tha
they feel more grateful toward others.

Initiating and writing such a diary can seem like a chore becaus
it is another thing to remember. However, once you get started
keeping your journal of what you are thankful for, you find that i

becomes precious to you. It is worth the time and effort. So, set aside a few minutes each evening and jot down those daily experiences for which you are thankful.

Gratitude Builds Friendships

Gratitude toward individuals, even when never directly expressed, creates a closer, higher-quality relationship. Gratitude brings a keen awareness of that positive value that your friends and family have in your life. This positivity matters immensely. You are more willing to put in that effort to maintain the relationship because you see how it influences you. You are more likely to treat these people better, which creates a better relationship. Your gratitude and that positive outlook create a more likely person to be liked and to befriend others.

Gratitude Inhibits Comparisons. One of the biggest threats to happiness are the individual comparisons that people make. When you compare your positivity to that of people around you, you can run into several issues. It is unfair to compare yourself with other people who have had very different life experiences and capabilities. When you do this, you invariably wound your self-esteem.

When you are grateful and live a life rooted in gratitude, you d not need unfavorable comparisons. Instead of focusing on how yo are doing worse than your neighbor, you value yourself based o how well you perform compared to yesterday or last year. You ca then reassure yourself that you are incredibly successful fc someone in your position based on your historical comparisor When you compare yourself to other people, you will never b satisfied. However, if you stop and are thankful for what you have you will stop envying your neighbors and build on the power c happiness.

Gratitude Diminishes Negative Emotions. Negativ emotions are threats to happiness. However, gratitude can help yo to fend them off. When you can be grateful to yourself and th world that you have, it dissolves negative feelings. You eliminat anger, fear, and other negative emotions. It is hard for you to fee angry or resentful when you think about how happy you are to hav what you have. It makes a great tool to use to keep your ow emotions in your control. If you want to be a positive person, yo embrace that positivity.

Gratitude Aids in Slowing Hedonic Adaptation. Th concept of hedonic adaptation, also known as "the hedoni treadmill," is studied by positive psychology researchers an others. It is a cyclical concept that refers to people's genera tendency to return to a set level of happiness despite life's ups and downs. Some activities seem to be more affected by hedonic adaptation, that the happiness they bring dissipates more quickly. These activities are known as pleasures, as they please in quick bursts, after which the feeling quickly disappears.

Gratitude fights against hedonic adaptation. Consider for a moment the honeymoon period in a relationship. It occurs when your relationship is brand new, and you are excited. You are happy. You and your new partner feel all of those hormones rushing throughout your bodies and feel the attachment and pleasant emotions. However, those are short-lived, and your body begins to adapt to them. That boost in happiness that you felt fades away rapidly because of the hedonic adaptation that you experience. Adaptation, while essential when you are dealing with negative situations, is harmful to positive feelings. One of the keys to mastering positivity, then, is learning to fight against that adaptation and developing your defenses, so the positive things in your life continue to bring you happiness, no matter how old they are. The best way to do this is through gratitude.

How to Master Gratitude

Gratitude Matters. We see this now. If you want to be happy person, you must be grateful. However, that can be challenge, especially if you have pessimistic tendencies. If you have found that your glass is always half-empty, it is time to look at what you can do to live a life filled with gratitude. It can be difficult a first, but the sooner you begin, the better off you will be. Let's go over ten simple actions to take in your own life to fulfill your sens of gratitude.

Thank Others Mentally. By silently thanking other people you practice for the real thing. Going through the motions wil trigger those feelings in yourself. If thanking others in real-time i too much, then do so silently. Think about how the people in you life who have helped you immensely, and focus on those points Focus on how you can recognize that these people have benefitted you so that you, too, can feel grateful toward the people in your life

Remember the Bad and Look at How Far You Have Come. The bad things in life will always be there. When something terrible happens, it leaves its mark. However, there is a benefit to this. You can look back at the bad when you surpass it. When you realize that life used to be so much more challenging and that you have done better, you have a reason to be grateful. This contrast is a great way to foster the gratitude that you may have missed.

Count Your Blessings. Regularly counting your blessings is an excellent way to make your gratitude habitual. When you count your blessings regularly, you are far more likely to succeed at maintaining your gratitude.

Prayers of Gratitude. Even if you are not religious, you may find benefit in using prayers of gratitude. These help you to recognize the connectedness in the world around you. It helps you think about what you are doing in the world around you, which is highly compelling.

Meditation. Meditation is the perfect opportunity to ask yourself what you feel grateful for. By reflecting upon the world and the gifts you have experienced, you can ensure that you feel more grateful over time. Remember to follow the steps in the previous chapter on meditation.

Questioning Yourself. There is a meditation technique known as *Naikan*. This process involves reflecting upon three questions, and the answers you discover to use to help you begin to feel more positive.

- What have I received from (person or the universe if you feel like being particularly reflective)?
- What have I given to (same person or the universe)?

- What struggles, problems or difficulties have I caused?

When you think about these questions and reflect upon them you can begin to do better yourself. You can see that you hav received for which it is worth being thankful. You can use tha thankfulness to determine what to do next. When you do thi enough, over time, you will realize that you probably have more t be grateful for in your life than you thought. If you are a naturall happy person, your focus on gratitude can help you feel happie than you usually would. If you are less happy or face many issues this extra attention to gratitude can help you live a more fulfillin life.

Visual Reminders. When you are trying to be grateful in you life, there are two common challenges that you will need t overcome to succeed. These are forgetfulness and lacking mindfu awareness. An excellent way to get around those impediments i through the use of visual reminders. Creating a visual reminder ca establish more of a gratitude habit. The visual reminder should b something that you see regularly, and it could even be a person When you have those visual reminders, you remember to b grateful.

Language Changes. By mindfully changing your language you can make yourself think more positively. Think of th difference between saying, "I have to go to work today," and, "I ge to go to work today." What strikes you as the most apparent difference between the two? The former makes work sound like a chore, while the latter looks at work as a privilege and conveys a sense of gratitude. By changing your language to be more gratitude-oriented, you can shift your focus to improve your happiness power. You want to look at everything as inherently positive and grateful.

Fake It Until You Make It. Finally, consider the art of just faking it. Go through the motions of being grateful, and your thoughts will eventually follow. Your body operates on a constant loop of thoughts, influencing feelings that influence behaviors, which once again influence thoughts. By changing your behaviors to be more grateful, even if you do not yet feel that way, you will discover that you can trigger that point. Smile at other people, and you will begin to feel happier. Write them letters of gratitude, thanking them for what they have done, even if you do not feel it is significant. Over time, the more you thank those around you, and the more you thank people for being there for you, the better you can make a change.

Summary

Frederickson's 2004 work on positive emotions revealed that gratitude leads to giving back to others, creating more opportunities for positive emotions and experiences to both the giver and the receiver. When you show appreciation for and return a kindness, you immediately increase your happiness level. Research has shown that people who live more grateful lives are happier, more satisfied, and less vulnerable to discomfort. Gratitude is inherently selfless. It is unconditional, and it shows your internal appreciation toward others.

Interestingly, gratitude is contagious, and it influences the well being of others. Studies have shown that gratitude is strongly related to happiness, positivity, better health, and better coping with stress and adversity. Happiness thrives in a state of gratitude. Gratitude helps you see yourself as better than you may have before.

Gratitude tends to encourage altruistic behavior. When you are grateful, you usually see that the good in life is external. Because of the reciprocity that gratitude often establishes, if you do a kindness for someone, they are likely to want to repay that act later with their gratitude.

It would help if you established a gratitude journal. Your gratitude journal is a diary of things for which you are thankful. Gratitude journals focus an individual's attention on the positive things. People who use them report that they feel more grateful toward others. The result is a happier person.

Gratitude fights hedonic adaptation. Research has shown that if you seek happiness, you must be grateful. Use the ten action steps you can take to fulfill your sense of gratitude.

As we continue the happiness power journey, a few more questions need answering. Why is self-esteem so crucial in establishing a happy persona? How is self-kindness related to happiness? These are just a few of the happiness questions we answer in the following chapter on the power of self-kindness.

By turning the page, you should already begin feeling better about your happiness powers and better about yourself.

Chapter 5

THE POWER OF SELF-KINDNESS

"To love oneself is the beginning of a life-long romance."

- Oscar Wilde

Two prisoners were sharing the same cell, exposed to the same set of circumstances.

The happy prisoner took pity and asked the unhappy one, "Why are you so sad?"

"Why should I be overjoyed, locked in these dank surroundings?" replied the unhappy prisoner. "I am so unlucky, as I was free just a few days ago. I was even basking in the sun at a resort, a much more exciting place than this cell. So why are you so happy as you are in the same disgusting cell as I am?"

The happy prisoner replied, "Just a few days ago, I was i another prison. You can't believe how bad it was there. Yuck! It like a resort for me here compared to the last place. Many othe prisoners want to get here, too, but I am the lucky one."

Situations are all relative and seen in comparison to each othe To be happ compare your current situation with a better one bu one that is worse. The moral of the story is that ultimately th decision to be happy lies within you. You have one life. You hav one body. You owe it to yourself to treat that life and body kind and with the reverence you deserve. Remember, no one will eve love or care for you like yourself, and you cannot give yourself t someone else to love you if you cannot love yourself first.

Self-kindness, an essential aspect of well-being and happines has been proven to help reduce stress. Self-kindness goes a lon way in developing two key traits that influence your happines self-worth and self-esteem. Your self-worth and self-esteem ar critical in making sure that you can achieve happiness in your lif yet so many people find that they cannot do so. Finding that powe of self-kindness is difficult if you have struggled with your sel worth. It can be difficult for you to tell yourself that you are vali and that you have worth. However, you are more valuable than yo realize. When you accept that you matter in life, you build on th power of happiness.

Being kind to yourself can come naturally to those people who think that they deserve it. For others, they may not believe that they deserve to treat themselves with the same patience, tenderness, and comfort that they might feel toward a loved one. Those individuals may have experienced childhood abuse or neglect that kept them from feeling kind toward themselves in much the same way that it may have been challenging to accept others' kindness.

Self-kindness is giving yourself the acceptance, patience, caring, and whatever else people use to define kindness. The definition of self-kindness also includes feelings of caring and comfort toward oneself. Most importantly, instead of self-criticism, self-kindness means being tolerant of our flaws and inadequacies. Unfortunately, it is challenging to treat yourself with kindness if you have not experienced much kindness from others. To develop self-kindness, you must learn the tools to support yourself when you experience failure or inadequacies.

Low self-esteem

Bear with me, as it seems I have switched subjects, but they are connected. You see, low self-esteem means you have negative thoughts about yourself—you do not love yourself. All those negative thoughts do is build unhappiness. But positive self-esteem means being more accepting of yourself and your life with fewe negative thoughts. You can be kind to yourself if you have health self-esteem and do more of the things you enjoy doing. It enable you to seek deeper friendships and feel comfortable in your skii Healthy self-esteem builds on the power of happiness.

We know that self-esteem begins in childhood. The voic through which you look at the world comes from the voice that yo heard as a child. Children who grew up with supportive, happy loving parents typically grow to have more self-esteem than thos who grew up with absent parents or parents who wer unsupportive or critical. Research has shown that the quality c parenting has directly influenced how children interact wit themselves, and because of that, we know that childhood matters

A recent study found that children have a sense of self-esteer comparable in strength to adults by age five. Self-esteem remain stable across one's lifespan, and thus the outcome suggests that thi important personality trait is already in place before children begi kindergarten. "Our work provides the earliest glimpse of ho preschoolers sense themselves," said lead author Dario Cvencek, . research scientist at the University of Washington's Institute fo Learning & Brain Sciences. However, just because you hav developed low self-esteem in childhood does not mean that you ar doomed to suffer throughout your adult life. There is no reason you must give in to the past and influence your future.

A recent analysis of many studies on self-esteem, using data from nearly 165,000 participants, concluded that self-esteem increases up to the age of sixty to seventy and then begins to decline. The reasons for this are found in the changes at various stages in development. For example, increasing self-esteem in adulthood is based on taking on new and more complex social roles. It follows that the loss of these roles in older age, such as retirement, widowhood, and so on, decreases self-esteem.

Ultimately, we are all worthy. We are all important in this world, and there is no reason that you should focus on putting yourself down. If you had critical parents growing up, you might have that sense of low self-esteem, but you can alter it. We will be looking at this issue in-depth.

Self-Esteem and Your Life

Self-esteem is an individual's subjective evaluation of their self-worth. It includes beliefs about oneself and emotional states like success, despair, pride, and shame. In their book *Social Psychology*, Eliot R. Smith and Diane M. Mackie define self-esteem by saying, "The self-concept is what we think about the self; self-esteem is the positive or negative evaluations of the self, as in how we feel about it."[3]

Self-confidence and high self-esteem are related to a successful life. The higher your self-esteem is, the more likely you are to succeed and create good relationships. You are more likely to be satisfied with life. These are significant factors that contribute to your happiness. You cannot be happy with low self-esteem.

With low self-esteem, you do not value yourself. You may find that you are depressed or unsatisfied in your life. You will find yourself struggling to meet your potential every time that you try to do something. Maybe you will even find yourself tolerating abusive relationships because you do not think you are worth more. You think that you are deserving of the abuse.

It is important to explain that the cure to low self-esteem is not high self-esteem. There is such a thing as excessive self-esteem. Overly high self-esteem prevents success or happiness. If you think too highly of yourself and your abilities, others will avoid you. It leads you to believe that the projects, tasks, or jobs other people propose are beneath you. That entitlement and an inability to learn from your mistakes can be incredibly off-putting. Many things can get in the way of your goals and happiness, such as low self-esteem and excessively high self-esteem. They are both equally bad. You must be able to navigate between the two extremes. When you find that middle ground, you will know that you have a healthy self-esteem that will maximize your happiness.

Determining Factors of Self-Esteem

One of the tools used in determining self-esteem is the Rosenberg Self-Esteem Scale, Devised by sociologist Morris Rosenberg. Researchers use the method for self-esteem research. It uses a scale of zero to thirty, where a score of less than fifteen may indicate a low self-esteem problem.

A few factors are involved when it comes to self-esteem. They will all influence how you see yourself. Your actions influence some of these. For example, you can choose to change how you see yourself and how you think. External forces set others, such as how people treat you. It is essential to consider that you have to know what creates it if you want to influence your self-esteem. When you can get that understanding, you will be able to take charge of yourself to establish a positive, healthy self-esteem.

Let's examine a few of the different influencing factors.

Your Thoughts and Perceptions. The thoughts and perceptions that you have about the world around you greatly influence your behavior. If you want to be happy in your skin, you want to make sure that your thoughts about yourself and how you

see your interactions with yourself are as positive as possible.
helps to make sure that you treat yourself with kindness. When yo
do that, your self-esteem will improve naturally.

How Others Respond to You. The way that other peop
respond and react to you will change how you think about yoursel
When people are kind or encourage us, we tend to feel mor
positively toward them. Alternatively, in a situation in whic
people are discouraging or make disparaging comments, we fee
worse about ourselves. Often, we look at what other people think c
us and influence how we interact with the world. It is why it is s
important to surround yourself only with positive people.

Experiences That You Have in Your Environment. Th
environment is also highly significant. Specific environments ar
more likely to create better self-esteem than others. In particula
you can see that positivity often links to growing up in a positiv
environment. The experiences that you have around you wil
matter. If you get positive feedback from your environment, yo
are far more likely to develop positive self-esteem.

Illness, Disability, or Injury. If you are suffering from
illness, disability, or injury that limits your ability to functio
normally, you may find that your self-esteem begins to wane. It i
a natural by-product of not being able to do as much as you onc

could. It is caused by struggling to do what you believe that you should be able to do.

Role in Society. The role you play in society varies greatly. In particular, people find that higher status individuals, such as those in leadership positions or positions of influence, tend to be much happier. Those who are in stable roles or positions feel more fulfilled and display higher self-esteem.

Media Messages. The media can also affect how you feel about yourself. The media sends all sorts of messages about what society wants from people. People start to confuse what they think society values rather than the values that the media portrays as attractive or desirable. The media tends to send an enhanced image. It is not focused on creating a realistic painting of what happens in life. Instead, it creates a situation in which you feel the pressure to live up to impossible standards.

The Link Between Happiness and Self-Esteem

Self-esteem and happiness connect in several different areas. Self-esteem influences and encourages happiness over time. When you have healthy self-esteem, you feel that power, and you find that you are happily able to be yourself, experiencing fewer problems.

You believe that you can be who you are without having to change yourself.

Keep in mind that self-esteem does not determine happiness. There is more to it than that. However, it is an essential building block to the house of happiness. It is especially true when you consider that low self-esteem is often associated with several negative thoughts. Because of these thought processes, you can usually find that you are happier with life when you are more accepting. Healthy self-esteem is a quality you should seek. With it you can be more resilient and to trust yourself. Positive self-esteem is essential to ensuring your happiness.

Self-esteem helps you to bounce back from rejection or failure by giving you resilience. It allows you to see the value that you possess despite any reversals. That observation is essential because it helps you to recover more quickly. Additionally, higher self-esteem reduces anxiety.

As with any feeling or emotion, self-esteem does not operate at a constant level: It fluctuates up and down. There are times when our self-directed goodwill deserts us. That is when we revert to remembering our faults. A cold, dank fog obscures our internal monologue, making for harsh judgments. The perspective change makes it easier to blame and shame ourselves for our torment.

One way to win back our aching hearts and reclaim our well-being is through self-compassion. This ideal borrows from Buddhist psychology. Self-compassion consists of treating oneself with kindness and care, just as we would treat a dear friend. One of the leading self-compassion researchers, Kristin Neff, has identified the three original parts of self-compassion: self-kindness, feelings of common humanity, and mindfulness.

While we see that self-esteem may help with happiness, it is not the entire answer. There is no single road leading to happiness. It is a complex highway system. Happiness is involved, with many factors influencing it. But research has shown that every little bit counts, and increasing one's self-esteem can make a big difference.

Signs of Healthy Self-Esteem

Before we begin to speak about building self-esteem, we will look at what healthy self-esteem looks like. When you can recognize what healthy self-esteem is, you can work on improving it. As you examine these points, see how related to happiness many of them are.

Being Authentic. When you are your authentic self, you can prove to yourself that you are more capable. When you are authentic, you are true to who you are. You are unabashedly willing to pursue and support your interests without guilt. It is essential t be happy. Authenticity and happiness go hand in hand.

Being Assertive and Setting Healthy Boundaries. Ther is a difference between aggressiveness and assertivenes: Assertiveness is fair and firm and recognizes boundaries that nee keeping so that one can remain respected. If you want respect, yo must establish firm boundaries. By being assertive, you can protec your happiness by maintaining that "line in the sand."

Not Worrying about Other People's Opinions. When yo have higher self-esteem, you do not care about other people' opinions. Any validation to your self-worth comes from withi yourself, which you can control and influence. It means that if yo need to maintain your self-worth, you can do so. Happiness come in this manner because you can create whatever kinds of interna thoughts you wish. You can remind yourself that you should thin in a certain way, and the only opinion that counts is your own.

Focusing on Yourself without Comparing Yourself t Others. Similarly, when you validate yourself without othe people's opinions, you can stop comparing yourself to others. W have seen several times that comparisons to others is a happines slayer. For this reason, high self-esteem is also indicative of greate happiness. When you see that you are your own person withou external validation, you stop basing your happiness on external factors and focus on yourself.

Not Worrying about Rejection or Failure. When you have higher self-esteem, rejection does not hurt as much. When you experience higher self-esteem, you allow your thoughts and opinions to influence you. You do not need someone else's actions to influence you. You stop worrying about what will happen if someone rejects you or changes your mind. You do not care about being rejected, and that is a freeing feeling.

Similarly, when you stop caring about others' opinions, you can also accept that failure does not matter as much. Failure is not the worst thing and does not need to be feared. In that state of mind, happiness becomes much more attainable.

Having Healthy Self-Talk. Using internal talk is an essential element when it comes to your happiness. If you want to be happier, you must be able to think positively about yourself. Having a healthy self-talk allows you to change the way that you think about yourself. Your self-talk convinces you that you are capable of more, and it acknowledges those abilities as positive. The result is a greater happiness.

Recognizing Positivity in Your Life. Positivity is everywhere in life. We know that positivity and happiness connect as well as positivity and self-esteem. When you have higher self-esteem, you can better cope with those failures in life and feel mor capable of accepting defeat.

Being Comfortable Being Alone. Because you will not b concerned about other people's opinions, you are comfortabl alone. When you can be alone without distraction, your happines becomes your own, and you need no one to validate you.

Meeting Your Own Needs Instead of Trying to People Please. Having higher self-esteem means you know that you hav a real, inherent value. Having self-esteem allows you to create you happiness. You will not have to worry about other people' opinions. You will meet your own needs instead.

Accepting Responsibility. When you accept responsibility you take control of your life. You must be able to accept tha responsibility if you want to improve your happiness. Remember When you acknowledge that you can control your life, you contro your happiness level. The more that you control, the happier yor are. As much as it can be unpleasant to acknowledge that you mad a mistake, reducing stress leads to improved happiness.

Showing Interest in Others as Well as Yourself. B shifting focus to improving your self-esteem, you can improv happiness. You can accomplish this by placing your interest ir people. It will help you to be more grateful. Helping others also improves your self-esteem and provides a sense of purpose

Volunteering or donating to a cause you care about or aiding someone in need of assistance boosts self-esteem and overall well-being. Helping others has an intense effect on brain chemistry; it creates joy and provides a sense of purpose, even in pain.

Forming Positive Affirmations. Positive affirmations are an excellent tool to help affirm your self-esteem. They work well by creating a sense of success and acceptance toward yourself. If you want to confirm that you are highly capable, then a fantastic starting point is introducing affirmations.

Affirmations are a pattern of acknowledgments that positively confirm personal values or beliefs. They are positive and personal statements that you repeat. The theory goes back to "fake it until you make it." The idea of an affirmation is that if you repeat it often enough, your unconscious mind will accept it. However, your affirmation must also be realistic. The affirmation that you create must be positive and capable of telling you what you need to hear. But it will not work if it is too unrealistically positive. You will not think about how accurate the affirmation is as it will be interpreted as mocking, thus becoming ineffective.

Identifying and Developing Your Competencies. We all have things in life in which we excel. Even if you do not think that you have any skills, if you look closely at yourself, there is always something that you can do better than others. When you list those things you can do, you can improve your self-esteem based on you competencies list. That is a beautiful way for you to change you focus toward the positive. What better way to make yourself happy

Frequently, when we struggle with self-esteem, we are quick t tell ourselves what we are incompetent. However, when yo identify and develop your competencies, you will recognize all th things you have accomplished. By recognizing that ability to d what you can do, you permit yourself to enjoy positivity an success. You teach yourself to talk to yourself in a kinder ton because you are competent and able to focus on the positive aspect of your capabilities and accomplishments.

Learn to Accept Compliments. Compliments are awkwar to accept for self-worth sufferers. How could you think that you ar worth those compliments when you think that you are unworthy Self-worth requires you to recognize that you are more than worth of those compliments, and it requires you to be willing and read to accept them.

Set a compliment goal. It is easy to do—make a game of it. Ever time a compliment comes your way, be strong, and accept with "thank you." Write them down and continue recording then (secretly, of course). Count the number of compliments you get i a day. At the end of two weeks, add the number together and savo the number you have received by people who value you. Trainin yourself to accept compliments will become a habit that will transform your esteem to the next level of self-worth. The goal is to accept the compliments that come your way. When you can accept them, you start to feel better about yourself, little by little. You can work with yourself to stop feeling so uncomfortable.

Accept and Reaffirm Your Self-Worth. Your real worth and your self-worth may not be adequately synchronized. However, as soon as you can begin accepting and affirming your self-worth, you will soon discover that you can be positive. By believing in the real value, you bring to the world, you successfully improve your self-esteem.

One of the best ways to accomplish this is by concentrating on the positive information you have created. Write down your positive qualities (yes, everyone has them). If a date has rejected you, write down everything about yourself that is particularly good on a date. The length of the list might surprise you and make you smile. If you are struggling to find a job, write out a list of traits that make you a great candidate. Then, when you have a list, choose something on it, and then write a quick paragraph or two about why that particular trait is so valuable and why you believe that someone will appreciate it. This exercise is surprisingly helpful and will make you feel so much better about yourself.

Eliminate Self-Criticism and Prefer Self-Compassion

Finally, reduce your self-criticism to help boost your self-esteem. When you can eliminate self-criticism, you find that you have another option: You can choose self-compassion. By eliminating self-criticism, you can treat yourself with kindness. That is because self-criticism harms your self-esteem. It leaves you feeling negative and unable to make progress in life. As a result, your self-esteem suffers. If your goal is to improve self-esteem, stay positive. Improvement will follow.

Summary

This chapter showed that self-kindness goes a long way in developing the two key traits that influence your happiness: self-worth and self-esteem. Self-kindness is giving yourself the acceptance, patience, caring, and whatever else people use to define kindness.

Self-esteem is an individual's subjective evaluation of their self-worth. It includes beliefs about oneself and emotional states including success, despair, pride, and shame. The higher your self-esteem is, the more likely you will succeed and create good relationships and a happier life. It is essential to build healthy self-esteem because it empowers you with the freedom to be kind to yourself and to do the things you enjoy doing. It enables you to seek deeper friendships and feel comfortable in your skin. Ultimately, we are all worthy. We are all important in this world.

One of the tools used in determining self-esteem is the Rosenberg Self-Esteem Scale. The factors that influence self-esteem include your thoughts and perceptions, how others respond to you, your experiences, illness, disability, injury, role in society, and media messages. Self-esteem and happiness combine in several different areas, but self-esteem does not determine happiness. While we see that self-esteem may help with happiness, it is not the entire answer.

You can improve self-esteem through affirmations. Affirmations are a pattern of acknowledgments that confirm personal values or beliefs. They are positive and personal statements that you repeat. Compliments are awkward to accept for self-worth sufferers. The sooner you can begin accepting and affirming your self-worth, the sooner you discover that you can be a more positive person, which in turn builds your happiness. We showed that if you reduce your self-criticism, you will improve your self-esteem. By eliminating self-criticism, you treat yourself with the kindness you deserve.

In the next chapter, we introduce the exciting concept of self purpose. We all want to find our purpose in life and understand the reason for determining how it relates to our happiness.

That raises the eternal question, "What is our purpose in life? It is not so easy to figure out your purpose in life. To answer the question involves answering other questions, including, "What does it mean to have a purpose?" We reveal the secrets of purpose in the next chapter. All you need to do to unlock them is to turn the page.

Chapter 6

THE POWER OF PURPOSE

"There's no greater gift than to honor your life's calling. It's why you were born. And how you become most truly alive."

-- Oprah Winfrey

There are times in life when we think that we would be happy if our dreams would magically come true. We know life does not happen that way. The effort that goes into achieving our dreams enriches us and makes us happy.

In this Sufi-credited story, a boy decides to reach for his dream. However, he lacks the strength, so he requests his father's help.

"Father. Can you help me?"

"Son, it would be my pleasure to help you, but I do not have such strength, as I gave it all to you."

The boy then asked the oracle.

"Prophet, answer my plea. Where can I find strength?"

The oracle responded, "The gods told me that I could fin
strength in the mountains of Tibet. Yet I couldn't find anythin
there, except the howling blizzards. And when I returned, the tim
away was lost forever."

He turned to the Sufi master.

"Holy Father, where do I find the strength to realize m
dream?"

"In prayer, my son. And if you find that your dream is not to be
you will understand it and find peace in your prayers."

The boy continued to ask everyone he met. However, the onl
consequence of his searches was utter confusion.

"Why are you so bewildered?" asked a wise soothsayer who wa
passing by.

"I have a dream, honorable, sir. But I don't know where to look t
find the strength to make it come true. I asked everyone, but no on
could help me."

"No one?" A light flashed in the eyes of the sage. "And did you as
yourself?"

That young man had not yet found his purpose until th
soothsayer's question triggered the revelation. The boy's strengt
and a sense of purpose were internal from the beginning. Thi

parable reveals that each of us has our sense of purpose inside, and when developed, we can achieve any goal.

Humans require purpose—it is one of our defining characteristics. We crave purpose, without which we would suffer serious psychological issues. Purpose is the fundamental element of fulfilling ourselves. Without purpose, we are vulnerable to boredom, anxiety, and depression.

Having a strong sense of purpose provides us with a positive, powerful effect. Armed with a sense of purpose, you can leap out of bed each morning, anticipating what is ahead for you in the day. You never wonder what you are going to do. When you focus on your purpose, life becomes more manageable and less complicated and stressful. You become single-focused, like a bright laser pointer, and your mind feels fully engaged, leaving no room for negative thoughts.

As Victor Frankl, an Austrian neurologist, psychologist, and Holocaust survivor, stated, "Those who have a 'why' to live by can bear almost any 'how.'" When you have a purpose in life, knowing that "why" will drive your success. You can get through even the hardest times and over obstacles knowing your "why."[5]

Individuals who can define their "why" can explain their motivation. Those who report that they have a meaningful purpose in life reported less pain (during a six-month study) than others who reported that they had not found their purpose. Purpose allows us to spend less of our time immersed in mental chatter, the phenomenon responsible for our negative thoughts and feelings.

The sense of purpose drives you forward in difficult times. It helps to remind you why those struggles are worthwhile and how you need to keep moving forward. In those moments, purpose protects you. In this chapter, we cover the power of purpose. We will examine why it matters and how purpose and happiness go hand in hand. If you want to be successful, you must develop purpose.

Why Your "Why" Matters

Your why is important for several reasons beyond providing drive and ambition. Your why allows you to understand what you are doing in life. Let's go over those reasons.

It Helps You to Stay Focused. Focus is imperative to finding happiness. You need to know what you want from your life. Keeping your eyes on the prize makes it easier to follow through with your achievements. To find happiness, follow your goals. It is easier than ever when you know why. You can let that why drive you forward.

It Makes You Feel More Passionate about Your Goal. By discovering your "why," you find your passion. You know what drives you, and knowing what drives you will point you toward your passion.

It Creates Clarity in Your Life. When you have a purpose, you feel unstoppable. It allows you to focus on the important and avoid time-wasters that do not add value to your life.

It Leaves You Feeling Gratified. Clearly defining what it is, that pleases you results in gratification. You will be able to use your "why" for better decision-making.

It Helps to Create a Value-Based Life. It allows you to live a life tied to the purposes that you established. By living by those values, you can improve your happiness.

It Allows You to Live a Life of Integrity. Integrity matters. When you live a life with integrity, you know what you want, who you are as a person, and why you do what you do. When you can identify your "why" in life, you can do more.

It Helps You Find Flow in Life. Those who discover their purpose operate in the flow of a stream of consciousness. They refrain from fighting against those things that happen to them; instead, they change themselves. They fight against fear and continually challenge goals.

It Makes Life Fun. Knowing your purpose allows you to enjoy life more. A purpose-driven life provides great pleasure. Even those tedious aspects of life are motivating.

Finding Your Purpose. In collaboration with University of North Carolina scientists, UCLA researchers have found that happiness derived from a sense of purpose in life has healthier genetic effect than pleasure-seeking. The desire appears to have evolved in humans to accomplish bigger and better things because it is closely associated with improved mental and physical health. As a result, it helps in our survival. A May 2014 study published in *Psychological Science* concluded that having a sense of purpose in life increases your life expectancy, no matter your age. Having a purpose in life appears to strengthen you against mortality risks across all adult years. Researchers are now studying whether having a purpose leads people to live healthier lifestyles which boosts longevity.

The goals established by our sense of purpose often change others' lives, such as establishing charities, disease research, and the Peace Corps, for example. This sense of purpose grows from our connection to others. There are many ways to formulate a sense of purpose in your life. What follows are the many ways to develop your own.

Explore Spirituality. Spirituality has relates to a sense of life-purpose for millennia. Research on spirituality has shown that people with a higher level had a greater sense of purpose. In a 2010 research paper, Leslie Francis studied nearly 26,000 teenagers throughout England and Wales. Francis concluded that Bible reading makes a small but unique contribution to promoting a sense of purpose in life among this age group.

Pursue Your Passions. Pursuing your passion is an excellent way to feel your sense of purpose. When we have something significant and enlivening to work toward, we will be more engaged and fulfilled by life's pursuits. In a March 2011 study, Raymond A. Mar, Joan Peskin, and Katrina Fong discovered a link between a passion for reading poetry and fiction and a sense of purpose among adolescents. Take stock of what you love and what you are passionate about—what makes you feel good. Then establish your objective to fulfill these goals.

Explore Your Values. Discovering what is essential in life assists in helping you find a sense of purpose. By discovering your values, you provide yourself with direction, which helps you live more intentionally. It improves integrity and aligns you to your beliefs. Your values are evident in relationships, career, spirituality, family, and finances, or more personal characteristics, like trust, reliability, humor, or courage. Living with a sense of purpose increases your well-being. If you are having trouble discoverin your purpose, find what you are passionate about and what yo value. Grow in spirit and attempt to connect with a higher being.

Know Your Superpowers. Everyone has a superpowe maybe even more than one. These abilities allow us to comple something with ease that others may find hard to accomplish. Th skill makes us stand out among our peers. When we practice th skill, it makes us feel fulfilled.

There are a myriad of books offering ways to better ourselve They suggest that we need improvement, although we tend t struggle with these suggestions needlessly. We do not need to b repaired or improved as these books suggest. Flaws and all, we ar perfect the way we are. The only thing we need to do is lov ourselves for who we are and recognize our skills for what they ar without further judging ourselves.

When we let our superpowers rest, we do not inspire ourselve We also feel drained when trying to use superpowers we do nc have. You cannot judge yourself for the lack of these power Instead, your task is to identify and use the powers you have.

Know Your Passion Moments. We all have those moment when we are doing something and do not realize that we ar working. They are those moments in your life when time seems t be standing still. When this happens, you are entirely in th moment. It is a flow state, a point in which you are completely engaged with what you are doing. These are highly powerful and influential moments. They tell you that you are doing something that was "meant to be." They provide that "aha" moment when you realize that you have found something about which you are genuinely passionate. For some people, it is working their dream job.

For others, it is creating something new or living a life with family. It is that moment in life when all is right when you feel empowered and passionate. Let those moments lead you. Let them drive you forward so that you are always on the right track. Allow them to provide meaning and recognize that they are pointing directly to whatever it is that creates that passion that you need to acknowledge. When you create that sense of passion, you know that you are on track to finding your purpose.

Listen to Feedback. It can be complicated to figure out those things that drive you and make you feel passionate. After all, you probably have dozens of things in the world that bring you joy and excitement. There are probably dozens of things that push you forward that make you feel happy. Listening to feedback—letting yourself hear what other people tell you—is a great way to figure out your passions. People are usually open to tell you what they think that you genuinely enjoy. They will not mind providing the feedback for you to use.

Start Conversations with Someone New. One of the best ways to identify your passion is to talk to someone you do not know. Take the time to hear them out, learn about them and what they like, and talk about what you like. As you do this, you may discover something new about yourself. You will be able to identify not only new things that other people enjoy that you may have never considered in the past, but you may also figure out your passions. Listen to what you talk about when you are getting to know these new people. It will relate to whatever it is in your life that drives you forward. You will be able to take and utilize that information. If you realize that you spent a significant amount of your time talking about politics, what does that mean for you? If you spend your time discussing your hobby of helping stray cats find new homes, maybe that is where your purpose lies. Your subconscious mind knows what your passions are, even if you have difficulty identifying them.

Explore Your Interests. Is there a topic that you find yourself looking at repeatedly? Is there something that you do regularly online or with your friends? Are you continuously volunteering to do something new or beneficial for other people, or are you chairing fundraisers to raise money for a cause that drives you? Take a look at your social media and scroll through your shared history. What do you notice? Is everything connected? If you are continually sharing videos and fundraisers about one or two topics, you can probably assume that those topics matter to you. In recognizing that they do, you can piece together how they may be passions of yours that are worth pursuing.

Consider the Injustices of the World That Bother You. Similarly, if you find that there are injustices in the world that get you fired up, analyze why. A lot of our deepest passions and purposes are tied directly to causes. Your passions are probably related to those causes you care about and hint about your purpose in life. You may not engage with them regularly, but if you find that you hear about human rights violations that set you off every time, that could be a passion point.

Discover What You Love to Do. Alternatively, you should also consider what you love to do. Look at what brings you joy. The passion point is to identify the connection between the acts you love to do and the topics that bring you the most energy and passion. When you find both, you are on the right track. All you have to know is what that point is.

Ask Yourself Questions. Asking yourself important questions that trigger your self-reflection is another way to identify

your purpose. These are four helpful questions that you ca
answer:

- What makes you come alive?
- What are your innate strengths?
- Where do you add the highest value?
- How will you measure your life?

When you provide the answers, you will better understand wha
you need out of life. You will recognize where your purpose lies.

The Purpose of *Ikigai*

In Japan, millions of people have *ikigai* (pronounced ick-ee
guy).[8] It is their reason to jump out of bed each morning.
translates to "reason for being." It is a process of balancing one
spiritual and practical life to an enjoyable lifestyle, one which i
also productive, the intersection between passion and talent. I
ikigai, there are four key concepts:

- What are you good at?
- What do you love?
- What can you be paid for?
- What does the world need?

These concepts interact: When what you are good at and wha
you love converge, you become passionate. What you are good a

and what you can be paid for creates your profession. What you can be paid for and what the world needs becomes a vocation, and what the world needs and what you love becomes your mission.

When your mission, passion, profession, and vocation all come together, you live a life of *ikigai*, of meaning, on a much deeper level. Ikigai is the best of all worlds, recognizing that it is entirely possible to find a point of convergence where you can have it all.

Finding that point of *ikigai* is essentially your key to living a life of your passion and purpose. It involves figuring out what you want to do with your life that will change the world while still bringing you great pleasure at the same time.

Finding that point of *ikigai* is to find joy and fulfillment in your life. It is to find a balance between the two and ensure that you can enjoy everything you do. It recognizes that you live a life in which you can be the you have always wanted. It involves making a difference in the world with your passions and encouraging you to become the person you were always destined to be.

Making Your Purpose a Habit

When you discover your purpose, you can elevate yourself further. You will be able to determine if the life that you live is beneficial to others. When you tap into that point, you have tappe the power to influence and control yourself.

Once identified, you can turn purpose into a habit. Now, you ar probably wondering what you could do to make your purpose int a habit. You can do a lot to make that happen. You must modif some of your day-to-day routines so that you can live a life c happiness. Here are some suggestions:

- Write visual reminders on notes, vision boards, o anything and the like to guide you daily.
- Make your new habit more compelling by sharing i with other people. Tell them that you are working o yourself and your habit and ask them for their support.
- Make your habit uncomplicated and easy to act on.
- Acknowledge when you accomplish a task.

When you make these little tweaks, you start to clarify tha living life according to those values will increase your happiness You become confident that you are making the right choices.

Summary

We examined why people require purpose. It is one of ou defining characteristics. Armed with a sense of purpose, you ca leap out of bed each morning, anticipating what is ahead for you in the day.

Individuals who can define their "why" can explain their motivation. It helps to remind you that those struggles are worthwhile and that you need to keep moving forward. The "why" is important as it provides your drive and ambition. It helps you to stay focused and makes you feel more passionate about your goal. It creates clarity in your life and leaves you feeling gratified. It helps to create a value-based life and allows you to live a life of integrity. It makes life fun. The goals established by our sense of purpose often change the lives of others, such as establishing charities, disease research, or supporting the Peace Corps.

Pursuing your passion is an excellent way to feel your sense of purpose. Discovering what is essential in life assists in helping find a sense of purpose. By discovering your values, you provide yourself with direction, which helps you live more intentionally.

Ikigai is a reason to jump out of bed each morning. It translates to "reason for being." It is a process of balancing one's spiritual and practical life in an enjoyable lifestyle, being productive at the same time. Where your mission, passion, profession, and vocation all come together, you live a life of *ikigai*. Finding that point of *ikigai* is to find joy and fulfillment in your life.

When it comes to happiness, the best way to achieve it is t
make sure that we are with other people. In our next chapter, w
answer the question, are family and friends important to ou
happiness?

So get in the mood by asking your best friend to help you tur
to the next page!

Chapter 7

THE POWER OF FAMILY, FRIENDS, anD COMMUNITY

"When you look at your life, the greatest
happinesses are family happinesses."

-- **Dr. Joyce Brothers**

J ohn Lennon, of the Beatles, related that when he was just
five years old, his mother told him that happiness was the
key to life.⁵ When John went to school, the teacher asked
everyone what they wanted to be when they grew up. When it was
John's turn to answer, he told her that he wanted to be "happy. "
She tersely replied that he did not understand the question. John
replied, rather cheekily, that she did not understand life. We all

know that John succeeded in his life's ambition, as he went on to make millions of us happy around the world with his original music.

Research has shown how our interactions with family and friends are the key to our greater happiness. Besides our family and friends, what about all those other people with whom we interact every day? The barista who smiles at you as she hands you your coffee; the man at the cleaners who tells you to have a beautiful day; the office secretary who nods to you as you walk by. Do those interpersonal actions increase your happiness?

In 1970, the sociologist Mark Granovetter examined people's social networks. He found that people's contacts separate into strong ties and weak ties. Strong ties are the connections that bond you with family, friends, and close work colleagues, whereas weak ties are connections with the people you see only occasionally. You do not have deep connections or regular contact with your weak ties.

Gillian Sandstrom and Elizabeth Dunn later examined whether weak ties contribute to happiness in a July 2014 study published in *Personality and Social Psychology Bulletin*. They found that the average daily number of interactions with strong ties was 6.7 whereas there were 11.4 interactions per day with weak ties. Further, they discovered that the number of interactions did not determine happiness directly. However, the number of interactions predicted the daily differences in the sense of belonging, which indirectly influenced happiness. In this case, strong ties were the most important determinant. When people had more interactions with their strong ties, they felt happier and had a greater sense of community belonging. Interestingly, the interactions with weak ties predicted a sense of belonging, but only slightly predicted happiness. The result was that more interactions with casual acquaintances increased the sense of community belonging but only had a weak relationship to increased happiness.

The study confirmed that the number of strong and weak interactions was related to the students' sense of belongingness. The more interactions a student had, the happier they felt, and the more they felt a sense of belongingness to the college community. When students interacted with close friends and less familiar acquaintances, they were less happy on days when they interacted less often.

According to researcher Emiliana Simon-Thomas, Ph.D., Science Director of the Greater Good Science Center at the University of California, Berkeley, "Human beings are an ultra-social species, and our nervous systems expect to have others around us."[9] Studies in biology, neuroscience, and psychology show that our bodies operate more efficiently when we're not alone.

Loneliness makes for poorer mental and physical healt outcomes. Lacking social support in your life lessens your abilit for happiness. According to Simon-Thomas, who studies th biology of our emotions and thinking. "We're built to seek out socia companionship and understanding."

Simon-Thomas elaborates, "Physiologically, not having a socia support system, is a chronic stress source for our bodies. Studie show that when people feel lonelier, they have higher levels of th stress hormone cortisol. And that type of chronic stress raises th risk of cardiovascular disease and other challenges to health an wellness."[10] Simon-Thomas describes that the relationship can als be an incentive for good behavior such as exercising and followin an improved diet.

There is no doubt that we all tend to seek interaction an relationships with others. A 2015 study published in *Neuron* foun that your brain operates more efficiently when interacting wit others and encountering rapport. The Finish co-authors reported "Social interaction is among the most complex functions humans and their brains perform. Yet, the interaction typically appear surprisingly easy."

Social baseline theory (SBT), the concept that integrates th study of social relationships with principles of attachment behavioral ecology, cognitive neuroscience, and perception science, suggests the human brain expects access to social relationships to make us happy.[10] As you have read and the studies conclude, interacting with friends positively impacts your physical and mental health. However, maintaining friendships is not easy. To further understand the value of friendships and how you might develop them, we discuss several helpful methods next.

The Benefit of Friends for Happiness Power

As we concluded previously, many studies have demonstrated that friends are beneficial to your health. Friends keep you happier during the good times and help lift your spirits during those low points. Of course, an essential mental health benefit of friendship is the elimination of loneliness. But friends can do so much more:

- They reduce your stress.
- They bolster your feelings of purpose and belonging.
- They can increase your happiness.
- Having friends improves your sense of self-worth and self-confidence.
- They assist you in coping with life's traumas, such as sickness, death, and divorce.

- Friends can encourage you to change your bad habit and build beneficial ones.

Friendship is downright healthier. Those with strong friendship reduce the risks of many health problems, including depression high blood pressure, and the tendency toward excess weigh Recent literature has reported that older adults live longer tha those without strong social connections.

Even though you can agree on the importance of friendshir initiating and maintaining friendships requires work. However, th benefit outweighs the work. In today's busy world filled with a those distractions, other priorities seem to get in the way. Change in your circumstance also alter the convenience of staying in toucl Even moving limits your ability to find ways of meeting new peopl and building new friendships.

Friendships are the golden opportunity to build on you happiness power. Keep your eyes peeled for the chance to improv on those you have.

Connecting with Friends

You may have overlooked the opportunity to see potentia friends camouflaged in the crowd. They are the people you alread know who travel in your social circle. Think of those people with whom you have interacted and who have made a good impression on you. You can develop deeper friendships among the people with whom you have:

- worked,
- attended classes,
- enjoyed speaking with at social gatherings,
- befriended in the past, and
- shared family ties.

For past casual acquaintances, set up your plan for anybody who stands out in your mind and who you want to know better and reach out. Reintroduce yourself by text, email, or, even better, an in-person visit. Then invite them for coffee or lunch.

Meeting new people to develop friendships takes more effort than renewing old friendships. To do so, you must visit locations where you might discover them, namely social events, grand openings, museums, galleries, and parties. You will gain more success, the more you attend.

It is easy to give up on this approach, but perseverance is a must as the effort does take time. Do not wait for the other person, or it may not happen. You have to initiate the invitation rather than waiting for invitations to come to you. Here are some excellen suggestions for your consideration.

Attend Community Events. Seek out clubs and events tha pique your interest or advance your hobby. You can find them liste online, at a hobby store, on supermarket bulletin boards, and i your local newspaper.

Volunteer. A great way to develop new friends is throug volunteering. Not only will you gain friends, you will also expan your sense of self-worth. Try the local food pantry, hospita nursing home, volunteer fire department, church or temple, c community center.

Extend and Accept Invitations. Do it the old-fashioned wa with handwritten invitations. Invite a friend to join you for coffe or lunch. Do not turn down invitations for social gatherings. Do nc forget to reciprocate when someone invites you to a gathering, o lunch, or dinner.

Take Up a New Interest. Try signing up for adult educatio classes at your library or community college. You will find peopl with similar interests there. You can find that the best reason t join a gym, health club, or YMCA is to build up your friendshi "strength. "

Join a Faith Community. Join a religious community or volunteer at your church or temple. Attend the meet-and-greet times after services.

Walk the Dog. If you do not have a dog, adopt one. Then you can meet dog-walking neighbors. With something in common, you can chat and head to the dog park for extended conversations.

Approach friend-making with an optimistic attitude. Maintain a cordial attitude; you will not be friends with everyone, but your attitude will eventually develop some best friends if you remain patient.

Bettering Your Relationships

It is not enough to have friends. Each of us must take responsibility for maintaining and reinforcing the bonds of our current friendships. If we neglect these relationships, they will slowly fade away, nurturing and cultivating your relationships if you want them to last. Here some great ways to do just that.

Spend a Sunday with Them. Find a Sunday when you are not doing anything and spend it with your friends. Both of you will feel closer to each other after spending the day together.

Be Comfortable in Silence. When you are comfortable in silence with the other person, you know that your relationship is blossoming. When your friendship deepens to the point of sitting in silence, you are building a closeness. Take the time to get to know others without feeling like you have to force a conversation. Let yourself be silent and feel how comfortable you can be.

Call Them for Advice. Everyone loves to give advice, so calling a friend for advice helps you both. You get the help, and your friend feels as if they have provided a good deed. It builds a closer friendship. So do not be shy when you need assistance. It is one way to deepen friendships.

Talk with Them. Similarly, if you want to better your life relationships, take the time to talk to the people who matter the most to you. When you do this over time, you will discover that you can deepen your relationship. The more you open your heart and talk to someone, the closer you become.

Read Each Other's Favorite Books. When you take the time to read each other's favorite books, you learn about your friend's interests. You get to know them better by enjoying something that you know they love. That will give a better insight into what is going on with them.

Pay Attention to the Little Things. Pay attention to what your friends and family members do. Do they have some sort of quirky coffee order that they like? Is there a reason that they do what they do? Learn those little things that your friends and family do that are unique to them, and then make it a point to remember their preferences. They will feel so much more appreciated when they realize that you are paying attention to their wants and needs. They will be flattered that you have paid enough attention and cared enough to notice.

Visit Them. You cannot have a good relationship with someone if you do not take the time to visit. You must spend time with the people around you if you want to better your relationships. Take a trip together. Invite them to hang out with other friends of yours. Whatever you choose to do, all that matters is that you get them involved.

With all those suggestions, you will create a budding friendship that will enhance your power of happiness and increase your life satisfaction.

The Importance of Community

Another road to friendship building is embracing your community. A comprehensive Harvard University study examined happiness over eighty years. In 1938, 268 Harvard sophomores had their happiness followed over their lifespan. As of 2017, only nineteen were still with us. The study extended to follow their children. The purpose was to understand how happiness influenced by time.

The study concluded that close relationships mattered the most for happiness. Some of the research participants became lawyers, doctors, and businesspeople, but, oddly, money did not appear to be the determinant of their happiness. Their happiness was related to closer relationships with people. The better one's relationships were, the more resilient they were against physical and mental decline. The quality of relationships became the best predictor of their happiness and success.

In June 2016, the University of Florida Survey Research Center polled five hundred Florida residents to learn more about their happiness and sense of community within the neighborhood. Those who were married, lived in a single-family home, owned a home, and had excellent health reported being very happy. Having children resulted in a slight decrease in happiness. The study found that individuals who have a secure connection to their community are the happiest.

However, the question is, do happy people seek out the social interaction and fellowship that are essential components of a healthy community? According to the study sample, the answer is yes. Those with a high sense of community reported being happy or very happy with their lives. This association indicates a powerful connection. Moreover, an analysis made to remove the effects of demographic variables showed that happiness alone accounts for 7 percent of an individual's sense of community. This sense of community influences the community's positive behaviors, such as volunteering and being a good neighbor.

Getting Involved in Your Community

With those studies in mind, you will want to be more involved with your community to earn more of your piece of happiness power. For that purpose, you need to have more interactions with the people who support your community. It adds to your sense of togetherness. Let's go over a few of the most critical considerations:

Get Involved with Local Events. What better way to get involved than to attend events in your area? When you see that there are neighborhood or local events, consider joining them. Have fun and support your local neighborhood or community.

Volunteer. When you are able, volunteer your time. In doing so, you ensure that your community is supported. It enables you to feel more connected.

Donate. By donating, providing resources that your community needs, you support it. By donating, you can help your community events or ensure that the people in your area get the help they need. Altruism leads to more altruism. When you are willing to help your community, your community will also help you.

Shop Locally. Support your local stores over shopping at chains. Keep your resources and money in your local community where it can recirculate.

Join Groups. When you become part of a team or a group, you can show you care about the people in your area. Taking the time to join in on the experimentation and festivities is one of the best ways to ensure that you are happy.

Support Local Sports Teams. Involve yourself in your community's passion and pride by supporting local sports teams. You probably have local teams, such as a town hockey or basketball team. If not, you can support the local high school teams.

Organize Events. By taking the time to create events, you can get other people involved. You can make the people in your area feel more connected than ever. By taking the initiative to start the events, you can show people for whom you care what you are doing and how you impact your community.

Summary

You can find happiness in many different, but perhaps one of the warmest ways is through friends and family. The number of interactions with these ties predicted the daily differences in the sense of belonging and happiness. The more interactions, the happier the study participants felt, and the more they felt a sense of belongingness to the community. That is because our nervous system is designed to function better with others around us. Studies in biology, neuroscience, and psychology have shown that our bodies operate more efficiently when we are not alone. Not having a social support system is a source of chronic stress for our bodies. Interacting with friends has a positive impact on both physical and mental health. Strong friendships reduce the risks of a large number of health problems.

Friendships are opportunities to build on your happiness power. Even though you can agree on the importance of friendship, initiating, and maintaining friendships requires work. Perseverance is a must when building friendships because the effort does take time. A great way to build friendships is through embracing community. A study found that individuals who have a secure connection to their community are the happiest. Those with a high sense of community reported being happy or very happy with their lives. You will want to be more involved with your community and build friendships to earn more of your piece of happiness power.

How does giving increase your happiness? In the next chapter, we will carefully examine the power of giving and how it adds to happiness power. It is not only an essential concept but can be fascinating personality characteristic.

Now on to the next chapter.

Chapter 8

THE POWER OF GIVING

"If you want happiness for an hour, take a nap. If you want happiness for a day, go fishing. If you want happiness for a year, inherit a fortune. If you want happiness for a lifetime, help somebody."

-- **Chinese Proverb**

In San Diego, forty people attended a special seminar on happiness. The meeting's leader asked the participants to write their names on balloons using a marking pen. An assistant then collected all the balloons and placed them in an adjacent conference room.

Once the balloons were safely ensconced, the attendees entered the adjacent room. They had to locate the balloons with their names on them within three minutes. There was an immediate scramble, and chaos ensued as the participants pushed and shoved to find their balloons. When three minutes had passed, not one balloon had been identified.

Then the leader asked the group to pick up any balloon and give it to the person whose name was written on it. After only two minutes had passed, everyone was standing there, holding the balloons with their names written on them.

The seminar leader spoke up, saying, "This exercise is an example of what is happening in our own lives. We are frantically seeking happiness, but we don't seem to know where to look." That is because the secret to happiness lies in the happiness of others—the happiness of giving. When you provide others with happiness, you will get your happiness in return. Pursuing happiness is the purpose of our lives. Give happiness to others, and happiness will surely follow you through life.

This chapter explains the relationship between non materialism and well-being. While we have explored studies in previous chapters showing that possessing wealth and material goods does not lead to happiness, it is time to examine how giving does.

Scientific research has provided compelling evidence to support the anecdotal evidence that giving is a dynamic pathway to personal growth and lasting happiness. According to the great Prime Minister Winston Churchill, "We make a living by what we get, but we make a life by what we give." Generosity is an essential characteristic of well-being.

Studies of volunteers have shown that they have better psychological and mental health and an increased lifespan. The benefits of volunteering on longevity outweighed exercising, attending religious services, and even giving up smoking. Another revealing study determined that when people received money, they gained more happiness when giving it away rather than using it on themselves. To them, happiness was more than just about feeling good. Their happiness was a result of a closer connection to others.

Clinical psychologist Seda Gragossian, Ph.D., of the Talk Therapy Psychology Center, said, "The key benefit of giving is that the individual turns away from their ego and focuses their energy and attention on someone other than themselves. Additionally, the act of giving forces one to focus on the present moment. I believe that's where the benefits of giving come from."[7] To be a giver is to be a person who finds happiness in helping others. To them, giving provides great pleasure and satisfaction and meaning. A study in the *International Journal of Happiness and Development* revealed how social connection helps turn generous behavior into positive feelings. Mahatma Gandhi once said, "The best way to find yourself is to lose yourself in others' service."[11]

Giving Leads to Happiness

Numerous studies have concluded that giving increase happiness in a much more beneficial way than receiving. In 2006 a National Institute of Health study found that our brain i activated when people donated to charity. This center correlate with trust, pleasure, and social connection. The researcher discovered that giving releases oxytocin and endorphins, the sam chemicals released when in love or breastfeeding.

In 2010, a Do Good Live Well study looked at 4,500 America adults who volunteered. They found that 41 percent volunteered a average of one hundred hours a year. Sixty-eight percent state that volunteering made them feel healthier. A total of 89 percen stated that it improved their sense of happiness. Seventy-three percent reported that it lowered their stress levels.

A three-university study on the emotional benefits of donating to charity was published in the *International Journal of Happines and Development*. Lara Aknin of Simon Fraser University led th study in Burnaby, British Columbia, Canada, and aided b colleagues at the University of British Columbia, Vancouver, and

Harvard Business School, Massachusetts. The study found that spending money on others or giving to charity leads to the most considerable happiness increase when giving encourages social connection. The exciting conclusion reported that donors felt happiest if they gave to a charity through a friend, relative, or social connection rather than merely making an anonymous donation to a worthy cause.

Absent the gift of money, the gift of time increased happiness when donating. A London School of Economics study found a noteworthy difference between the happiness of volunteers and non-volunteers. The study concluded that happiness levels surged the more people volunteered. Their happiness increased 7 percent for a monthly volunteer, and for a weekly volunteer, their happiness rose 16 percent.

The primary characteristic of giving is its potential for creating powerful social relationships between individuals and groups. Giving has long-lasting effects throughout a lifetime. Giving is contagious, inspiring the receiver to return the favor. As giving increases, so too does happiness.

Altruism is the glue that binds families and social groups together, helping them to cooperate and thrive. In their 1996 study, Trudeau and Devlin concluded that introverts and extroverts might be highly altruistic and actively engaged in many types of volunteer work. Still, the motivation may be different. Following that study research in 2001 by Krueger et al. found that altruism links t shared familial environments, unique environments, an personality traits that reflect positive emotionality. Individual who live in positive family environments with constant suppo tend to be more generous than individuals who live in advers family environments.

Activates the Brains Reward Center. A June 2007 study conducted by Professor William T. Harbaugh and his associate (from the University of Oregon), concluded that charitable givin creates a brain response that imitates ones activated by drugs an other stimuli. This reaction initiates a surge of dopamine an endorphins. Charitable giving can induce happiness in the deepe part of your brain, more so than physical pleasures.

Improves Life Satisfaction. A December 2007 Germa study provided ample evidence that "givers" of time and materia things experience greater satisfaction in life than those who do no The same holds for generous communities. Those who are giver demonstrate greater satisfaction within the community tha groups of people who do not give. The moral is that you are happie living in a generous community than one that is not.

Feels Happier. Satisfaction and happiness are two differen emotions. Researchers from the University of Missouri and th

University of California, Riverside, found that those who gave others scored higher on feelings of joy and contentment than individuals who did not give to others.

Just Thinking About Giving Can Make You Happy. In a study published in *Nature Communications*, researchers reported they discovered that even thinking about doing something generous has real mood-boosting benefits. The University of Zurich revealed to fifty participants that they would be receiving one hundred dollars throughout several weeks. Half of the participants spent the money on themselves, while the other half were requested to spend the money on someone they knew.

The purpose was to determine whether the promise to spend money on others was enough to make them happy. Before handing out any money, the group received instructions to think about the person they would like to spend on and how much they would spend on the gift. They received a magnetic resonance imaging scan of three regions of the brain associated with social behavior, generosity, happiness, and decision-making.

The giver participants made more generous decisions during the experiment than those who had agreed to spend on themselves. They also demonstrated more interaction between the parts of the brain associated with altruism and happiness. The anticipation of giving benefitted the givers by providing them with higher happiness levels when the experiment concluded.

The study's leader, Philippe Tobler, associate professor of neuroeconomics and social neuroscience, reported, "It is worth keeping in mind that even little things have a beneficial effect, like bringing coffee to one's office mates in the morning."[12] If you are about to buy yourself a treat to make you happy, the Tobler study concludes you should do the opposite. Buy someone else the treat and you will feel happier. At least think about it. "It is worth giving it a shot, even if you think it would not work," Tobler said." To reap health benefits, repeated practice is probably needed so that giving becomes second nature."[13]

By being generous and giving to other people, you are benefiting yourself rather than the receiver. That allows you to feel the enjoyment of helping. Besides the happiness it provides you, it is a powerful method to build self-worth and self-esteem.

This concept is true whether you are donating time or money. A powerful way to deal with depression is by volunteering. It enables you to see how you are needed and how others value you. This theory holds whether you are giving money, gifts, or time. Feeling the impact of giving and making a difference provides an instant happiness injection. You will be improving yourself and the others you are helping, an excellent formula for happiness power.

The Cost-Benefit of Giving

Generosity is not necessarily a natural choice, as there is a cost to a selfless act. When you give to someone, you are giving your time, money, and resources. A 2017 study led by Professors Phillipe Tobler and Ernst Fehr (Department of Economics, University of Zurich) focused on understanding what happens in the brain during a generous act.

They used magnetic resonance imaging to research how generosity influences happiness. To incentivize altruistic behavior, the researchers used the method of a public pledge. The researchers informed the group that they would receive envelopes of money. The experimental group was required to spend their money on other things besides themselves over four weeks. The other half of the group were required to spend the money on themselves over the same period.

Surprisingly, the researchers found that the participants spending on others were likelier to purchase gifts at a higher cost. That is, they were more charitable and generous than the participants in the control group. The participants opted to act more generously despite the costs. The reason was probably motivated by the prospect of the "warm glow" provided to the givers.

According to Professor Tobler, "Our study shows that even in strictly controlled laboratory setting involving decision-making i the [magnetic resonance imaging] scanner, commitment induce generosity along with increases in happiness. You don't need t become a self-sacrificing martyr to feel happier. Just being a littl more generous will suffice."[14]

Simple Ways to Give

When it comes to increasing your power of happiness, there ar many ways to do so. Giving does not have to be grand or elaborate— even just a giving smile is a start. Let's go over some of the way that you might consider.

Spend Money on Others. The most traditional givin involves spending money on other people. Even a small gesture lik buying someone a pack of gum or a lip balm can increase your sens of happiness.

Spend Time on Others. Volunteering your time or spendin time with someone is often a more thoughtful gift than spendin money on the person. Time is a beautiful gift to give.

Volunteer. Volunteering is like donating your time. You ar giving something up to whatever cause you are supporting, and yo do not have to reach for your wallet to do it.

Be Emotionally Available. Listen and be available to those who need your help. If someone asks to sit down and talk to you, then do it. If they want to spend time with you, then do so. It is one of the best things that you can give—your emotional support matters.

Perform Acts of Kindness. Random acts of kindness are great for bettering yourself and those around you. Hold the door open for someone, let someone cut in line, help someone with their bags; you know what to do to make you both feel happy.

Compliment Someone. Tell someone that they look good or have done something well. A few kind words that will not take anything out of you.

Make Someone Laugh. You can also give someone the gift of laughter. What better way to bring happiness than to make someone laugh? By doing this, you can give someone a gift that they cannot deny, and in doing so, you know that you are providing the kindness they need.

Tell Your Story. Sharing your experience is one of the greatest gifts you can.

Meaningful Ways to Help Others

Being generous with our time and talents increases ou
happiness power and builds our prosperity. When we volunteer ou
services to others, the payment received is broad smiles, warm
thank-yous, sincere gratitude, and a sense of purpose. That is wh
we want to share the six tips on helping people more effectivel
with you. You will be in higher service to those around you whil
stocking up on your happiness power by employing them.

Sharing Knowledge. When you share knowledge with thos
around you, they can learn from you. You grant other people you
expertise and experience, and there is power in that.

Finding Out What Other People Value. When yo
discover what other people value, you might be able to it.

Sharing Your Resources. Your resources are your currency
Select which of them you can share with other people. For example
if you have extra food, you might choose to share it with you
neighbors. When you win an extra set of tickets that you do no
need, give them to your friends. Sharing those resources will bette
your relationships and make you feel good about yourself.

Give Feedback. When you give people feedback, you tell them
what they could do to make genuine change. Transparent feedbacl

is painful at times because constructive criticism is rarely well-received. So be tactful.

Sharing Opportunities. Sometimes, you may become aware of a privilege, and if you can share that awareness with other people, you help them better themselves. Pass on potential opportunities, such as job availability, a grand opening, a new play in town, and so on.

Recognizing Someone's Achievements. Taking the time to congratulate someone on a job well done is a wonderful way of validating another person.

Protecting Yourself from Being Taken Advantage of

To maintain your happiness power, make sure that you do not overextend your giving. You do not ever want to give so much that you regret what you have done. Here are a few cautions to follow to avoid gifting burnout.

Find Your Passion. Ensure that your passion is at the heart of the giving. Give to the areas for which you are passionate. Give your time; donate selectively and with thought. You also need time for your work and yourself, so manage your time well.

Find a Way to Integrate Your Skills and Interests with Others' Needs. Look for those opportunities where your skill set

can dovetail with an unfulfilled need. For example, if a welder i
finishing a job and a neighbor needs a metal railing repaired, th
tools are available.

Be Proactive. By choosing to take action and determine whe
you want to do something, you can better plan your time.

Do Not Fall for Guilt Trips. You do not owe anyon
anything, so avoid those who try to manipulate you. You do nc
have to do something that makes you uncomfortable. That is nc
how to acquire happiness power.

Adopting an "Others" Mindset in Your Daily Life

Giving and altruistic behavior is not always easy to achieve
However, if you allow the power of empathy to work, it ha
unexpected consequences. The Native American aphorism goes
"Before you judge a man, walk a mile in his moccasins." In effect, i
is a reminder to practice empathy. By practicing empathy, you giv
yourself the ability to live a "giver's" life. If you can put yourself i
the other person's shoes, you will understand why their world is nc
as easy as you think. Fortunately, one can learn empathy. Take
look at suggestions that can help you reposition your mindset to b
a more generous "giver."

Take Time to Spend with Others. Make a conscious effort to spend time with other people. Your happiness relates to the way that you interact with others.

Listen Well. Listening to what someone else has to say is not always easy, but the other person appreciates it. Be a good listener and take everything your friends and family have to say to heart.

Make Someone Else's Day, Every Day. Have a plan to make sure that you do something to make someone else's day, from a compliment to buying lunch. It will build the happiness of two people.

Summary

The old saying, "It is better to give than receive," has been proven in numerous research studies. Giving does increase happiness in a much more beneficial way than receiving. In 2006, a National Institute of Health study found that a specific brain area was activated when people donated to charity. Absent the gifting of money, the gift of time increased happiness when.

We found that giving has the potential to create powerful social relationships between individuals and groups. We also found that altruism is the glue that binds families and social groups together. A University of Oregon study concluded that charitable giving creates a brain response that imitates those activated by drugs and other stimuli. A German study provided ample evidence that "givers" of time and material things experience greater satisfaction than those who do not.

Generosity is not necessarily a natural choice, as there is a cost to selfless acts. When you give to someone, you are giving your time, money, and effort. There are many ways to give to increase your happiness power.

To maintain your happiness power, make sure that you do not overextend your giving. You do not ever want to give so much that you regret what you have done. Giving and altruistic behavior is not always easy to achieve. However, if you allow the power of empathy to work through you, it has unexpected consequences.

In our next and final chapter, we ask how to break through those barriers that are blocking your happiness? We provide some surprising answers.

So, hurry now, and turn the page!

Chapter 9

THE SURPRISE ENDING

"Happiness is not something ready-made. It comes from your actions."

-- Dalai Lama

O nce there was an older man who lived in a rural village. He was one of the most wretched people in his country. The entire village disliked him, as he was joyless, always lamenting his situation and never in a pleasant disposition. The longer he lived, the worse his temper grew, and the more treacherous his words. The villagers learned to stay away from him because his misfortunes were so infectious. One could never be comfortable in his presence. He inspired unhappiness in all who would meet him.

But on his seventy-ninth birthday, a remarkable transformation took place. The gossip around the village quickly spread. "The old man is happy today!" Sure enough, the villagers witnessed the startling change. He stopped complaining. He began smiling, and they could hear him chuckling to himself.

One brave villager dared ask, "What is wrong with you?"

The old man answered, "Everything is right with me. For seventy-nine years, I have been seeking happiness, and it was elusive. Yesterday for my birthday, I decided to live the rest of my life without looking for it and enjoying the years I have left on this Earth. That is why I am happy now."

The Happiness Conundrum: More Is Less

Pursuing happiness is one of our primal instincts. It is an underlying motivator: the pursuit of physical pleasure, our desire to avoid pain, our need for emotional pleasure, and our desire to avoid emotional pain. The need for emotional enjoyment or happiness is a basic human desire.

Achieving and creating happiness is not accomplished the way we think. Our common sense has us believe that pursuing external things obtains happiness. In other words, it is happiness by accumulation. Therefore, to be happy, we seek a better job, an attractive partner, more money, a fancy car, a better body, others' opinions about us, how many "likes" we get on social media, and so on. However, the research we have examined so far tells a different story. It seems to contradict our common sense because all the studies conclude that real happiness is not found outside ourselves in the material world; instead, it is found within us. To create and live in authentic happiness, you will need to embrace the happiness truth—like the old man in the story—and not chase those false beliefs.

With the natural desire to be happy, have you considered what concentrating on happiness does to people? Researchers have studied this phenomenon. To their surprise, they discovered that as we place more importance on being happy, not only do we become less happy, but we become depressed. In other words, the emphasis on the search for happiness results in more unhappiness. Arranging your world around your attempts to be happy or making happiness your goal for happiness's sake impedes your happiness.

In one study, those participants putting the most emphasis on being happy reported 50 percent fewer positive emotions, 35 percent less satisfaction about their life, and 75 percent more depression than people who focused elsewhere. The study concluded that the more people pursued happiness and organized their life around attempting to be happy, the less happy they ended up.

In a second study, participants had to read two versions of a fake news article concerning happiness and its scientific value. I incorrectly reported that those experiencing the most happiness achieved long-term benefits in their life. Half the participants read the article about happiness, while the other half read a similar article without describing "happiness." The researchers then had both groups watch a comedic movie. When provided with the happiness benefits article, those participants enjoyed the movie less. That is, participants conditioned by happiness benefits were less appreciative of positive events.

This happiness reversal may not be so surprising, as the ancient Greek philosopher Plato, around 300 BC, had put his finger on the problem. He observed, "The excessive increase of anything causes a reaction in the opposite direction."[15]

Happiness Is Achieved Indirectly

Aristotle, a student of Plato, believed that happiness is about living an enjoyable and meaningful life. He wrote that happiness is much more than a temporary pleasure found and lost in a short time. According to happiness is achieved indirectly. He proffered that it results from a life well-lived and that those tempted by life's pleasures would not end well.

Aristotle's philosophical idea of happiness was reintroduced to modern social science by Dr. Martin Seligman, the founder of positive psychology, which we discussed in Chapter 1. Seligman authored the book *Authentic Happiness*, which established the field. He used the word authentic to distinguish happiness from pure pleasure. According to Seligman, authentic happiness is achieved by cultivating "strengths of character" ("strengths" being a term for virtues).

Working with Dr. Seligman, Dr. Chris Peterson led a forty-person research team to study character and its manifestations. Dr. Peterson put the research results in his eight-hundred-page book, *Character Strengths, and Virtues*. This book explains that: "Twenty-four character strengths are evident in human history. Evidence of all twenty-four strengths exist throughout all cultures of the world. All twenty-four character strengths exist in every individual; they range from bravery and forgiveness to integrity and gratitude. These character strengths are the foundation of the Positivity Project's model. "

Character Strengths Required to Achieve You Happiness

The science of positive psychology has narrowed down th twenty-four character strengths that Dr. Peterson identified in hi study to five character strengths connected with the highest level of happiness. These numerous studies confirmed that the fiv strengths were happiness strengths:

- Zest
- Hope
- Gratitude
- Curiosity
- Love

VIA Character Institute research has confirmed that over 75 percent of people have one of these strengths in their top five.

American novelist Nathaniel Hawthorne famously said, "Happiness is a butterfly, which, when pursued, is always just beyond your grasp, but which, if you sit down quietly, may alight upon you."[12] Here is the explanation of the activities that will build your character strengths and generate the butterfly attraction to compel it to land softly on your shoulder. The five exercises are guaranteed to boost your happiness levels rapidly.

Zest. Zest refers to movement and activity. To increase your zest, get out and get moving: Plan an exercise routine, walk the dog daily, or participate in a sport. Move because movement increases your energy levels and produces the endorphins needed for well-being and good health. Why zest? When you use your zest character, you are enthusiastic and excited about what is going on in your life. You are doing what psychologists call *behavioral activation* because you are lifting your energy levels by taking action with your body and mind, not to mention your happiness.

Hope. To boost hope requires a bit of projection. Imagine yourself a year from now. Where do you want to be? In what activities are you participating? What are your goals and dreams? Write these down because writing about them helps with a clear visualization. It will allow you to move from thoughts to actions. These possibilities are your hopes for the future. Why hope? Being hopeful inspires optimism about a future event. In this case, they are the goals you have written. When you are hopeful, you are not easily discouraged and can find alternate pathways to achieve your goals. Hopeful people display confidence and motivation, which leads to increased happiness.

Gratitude. Give thanks to others daily. Write an email or a letter to someone you are grateful to—a person who has recently impacted your life but whom you have failed to thank. Correct that now. Use the phone to make a few thank-you calls. Your thoughtfulness will create happiness in you both. Why gratitude? Expressed gratitude realigns our thinking and changes how we feel. We shift into a positive emotion and expand our feeling about others. Gratitude reconnects us with others and reminds us of our community of support. It reinforces our positive relationships, which indirectly delivers happiness.

Curiosity. It is the practice of reverse switching. Chose an activity that you are not fond of: Perhaps it is raking leaves or ironing clothes. When you find yourself engaged in your unpleasant activity, concentrate on three attractive features of that activity. For example, think about the sun's warm feeling on the back of your neck or the scent of cinnamon and spices coming from a leaf pile. Listen to the sweet crunch of the leaves under your feet. You get where this is going. Be positive with your curiosity. Why curiosity? By exercising our curiosity, we can find new and different pursuits. With this new effort, we can explore our world, ourselves, and other people. It leads us to discovery and personal growth, and a greater sense of well-being. With well-being, happiness follows.

Love. Start a loving-kindness (metta) meditation. Keeping your eyes closed, think of a person close to you who loves you very much. It could be someone from the past or the present, someone still alive or who has passed. It can be a spiritual teacher or guide.

Imagine that person standing on your right side, sending you their love. That person is sending you wishes for your safety, for your well-being and happiness. Feel the warm wishes and love coming from that person toward you.[13] Repeat the following phrases silently:

May I/you be filled with loving-kindness.
May I/you be safe from inner and outer dangers.
May I/you be well in body and mind.
May I/you be at ease and happy.

This type of meditation connects you with many physical and psychological benefits. Why love? The strength of love involves both the giving and receiving of warmth and closeness with others. It is the foundation for building healthy, positive relationships, which researchers view as one of the best pathways for boosting our happiness.

Butterfly Bait

If you are too focused on chasing happiness, you might end up chasing it away. In John Kay's book *Obliquity: Why Our Goals Are Best Achieved Indirectly*, the author believes that the best things in life arrive indirectly. Suppose you want to experience fulfillment and well-being. In that case, you need to shift your goal toward those projects and relationships that bring fulfillment. As the nineteenth-century philosopher, John Stuart Mill wrote, "Those only are happy who have their minds fixed on some object other than their happiness."[18] What follows are some indirect but proven exercises you can practice to attract the happiness butterflies.

Become Familiar with Your Story. You cannot hope to improve your internal story that you tell yourself until you identify it. Casandra Brené Brown, Ph.D., LMSW, a professor at the University of Houston's Graduate College of Social Work wrote, "Owning our story and loving ourselves through that process is the bravest thing we'll ever do." She calls this story your SFD, or "sucky first draft." She advises that you think about the story without judging or analyzing it and then write it down in bullet points. Once written, examine what pieces are facts and what are the assumptions.

Reverse Your Story. An excellent method to help yourself is by turning the story around. Concentrate on the language you are using to tell yourself the story and then reverse it. For example, if you hear, "My boss doesn't value me," you can reverse it, saying, "I am valuable at work because I catch all his errors for him." Another example: "I am ignored" can become "I am valuable."

Connect Yourself to the Future. Try this: List all your successes. List those things that have brought you joy. Honor and give thanks for those things. Now ask yourself, "What made those things possible?" and, "How can I experience more of these kinds of successes?" You can also ask, "What bigger successes do I want, and how can I create them?" Focus on bringing those things to fruition and repeat those questions to yourself often.

Experience Meditation. Our inner dialogue is almost instantaneous. It begins when we least expect it. Building a habit of meditating for just ten minutes can significantly slow your thoughts and stop any negative stories before they take hold.

Determine What Makes You Happy. Most of us do not know what makes us happy because we tend to focus on material things. Thus, we should take time to think about the non-material items that are fulfilling. Find the current opportunities in your life and the things that interfere with your ability to do them. Think about past negative experiences, and then retell the story that you would like to experience.

Be Grateful for Today. Starting your day with a "thank you" puts you in a state of gratitude and brings more joy and things for which you can be grateful. It works like magic. We can attract joy and happiness or sadness and despair. To reinforce that, note three things you are grateful for every day, even if it's food. As soon as you write it down, you will start to feel happier.

Visualize Life as a School. See life as a high school with many subjects to learn—not a test of your values. Thus, your errors and life lessons do not affect your value. Simply shift your thinking on how you feel about a subject.

Be Your Own Best Friend. Words are often hurtful. Stop being unkind to yourself and putting yourself down. Use only positive words when you speak to yourself. They will be empowering and fulfilling.

Pause When You Notice Yourself Being Negative. From this moment on, promise yourself that you will stop your negativity. Choose a new approach that brings joy into your life. Own your power to choose.

Connect with People Who Support You. See yourself through their eyes. The reminder may help you reconnect with yourself when you felt more passionate and joyful, and you can use that feeling going forward.

Now that you are familiar with the indirect approach for attracting happiness to your life, we want to offer a few things to do when you catch yourself in a state of unhappiness. No one's happiness is constant—we all find ourselves in unhappy moods at times. The following methods can quickly reverse the unhappy thoughts.

Add a "But" to Turn Your Unhappiness Around

When you find that your thinking turns to a negative mindset, do your best not to dwell on it. "I'm failing at my goals," you might say. "I'm not getting good grades." "I'm not able to be the person that I want to be right now." No matter what you do, however, cease negative talk. The next time you find yourself talking about how unhappy you are, add a "but" to the sentence. "I'm so unhappy with what I am doing, but I'm healthy." "I'm not pleased with the work that I'm doing today, but I know that I'm trying my best and that matters the most." When you start to turn things around with this positive language, you realize that you do not have to let yourself be a slave to that negativity.

Stop Making Meaningless Affirmations. So many people use affirmations that they think will help them, but they chose the wrong structure. If you find that you are continually trying to create new affirmations that just are not cutting it, follow a different format. Instead of, "I'm a positive person," which might not be enough for most people in their journey toward happiness, you can say, "I choose to be happy." You make your affirmations stronger when using this format, and that makes all the difference.

Memorize a List of Happy Words. When you have a list of positive, happy words that you use to describe yourself and those around you, you realize that you can improve your self-talk. Instead of letting negativity rule your life, using positive talk with an improved vocabulary will be beneficial. Memorizing positive language will aid you in changing how you speak about yourself. (See the list of happy words in the Appendix.)

Use Associations to Bring Happiness. Sometimes, the best way to make something a positive habit is to make it a point to do something. Remind yourself through associations that you can do better. For example, perhaps you need to improve your mood, but you because you have negative thoughts. Choose something as a trigger for something positive. A common one is that you must think of three positive things when you get into your car, or you could choose to make your computer, your phone, a pen, or anything else a conduit for your positivity. Every time you see the item of choice, make it a point to say a few positive things about what is happening before moving on. Doing this will establish a happy habit and improve your mood.

Actively Gravitate Toward Things That Bring Happiness. Finally, one last tool that you can use to ensure that you are attracting happiness is gravitating toward it. Make a list of those things that bring you happiness. The best life that you can live is one where you find ways that will help you to discover happiness. When you know that there is something that you enjoy, make it a point to value it. If you find true happiness in helping others, live by that. By being passionate about the things that bring you happiness, you will live a meaningful life.

Conclusion

Questions, questions, and more questions. Why is happiness considered a vital component of life, especially when there are many aspects to a fulfilled life? Can individuals learn to be happy? Is happiness a choice? Does happiness provide power to those who experience it? How can you be happy? This is what I attempted to answer in this book.

We examined the many happiness studies in detail and concluded that happiness seems to be the priority that people aspire to achieve among the many emotions we experience. Happiness provides significant powers to those who experience it. There are a minimum of fifty powers created when experiencing a state of happiness.

We looked at the relationship between optimism and happiness. Having an optimistic approach to life is critical to attain happiness. An optimist expects more positive things to happen than negative ones. A September 2019 study suggests people who tend to be optimistic are likelier than others to live to

ROBERT GILL JR.

be at least eighty-five years old. Now that is a power we all wish to experience! Compared with pessimistic people, optimists are more successful in school, at work, and in athletics. They are healthier, live longer, and are more satisfied with their marriages. They have better mental health, are less anxious, and are less likely to suffer from depression.

We dispelled happiness's biggest misconception. Happiness does not depend on what we have; it depends on how we feel toward what we have. We can be happy with less and miserable with more.

Studies have shown that happiness provides the power to boost motivation, creativity, and energy. It improves productivity, and research indicates that happiness gives people greater power over their physical health. Happiness is also contagious. Happy people inspire those around them by elevating their mood. Yes, the power of happiness can seem magical. The fifty powers of happiness list divides into physical powers, health powers, mental powers, workplace powers, and social powers.

Researchers think of happiness as having meaning and satisfaction in one's life. It identifies with positive emotions and rapidly recover from negative emotions while experiencing a sense of purpose. Its chemistry is little more than impulses in the brain loaded with chemicals known as neurotransmitters.

Studies have found that we are happier when we live fulfilling lives. Material wealth does not bring us fulfillment. Happiness is a learned emotion, even though there is some individual genetic predisposition.

Happiness has a significant influence on good health, just as good health influences happiness. Happiness is a critical health factor during difficult times. According to Yale psychology professor Laurie Santos, finding happiness during difficult times matters. Dr. Santos found that happiness gives us the power to get through. Happiness and physical health have been connected for a long while. We examined whether happiness has the power to improve physical health or if physical health creates happiness.

We also looked at the flip side of happiness. We found that negative emotions are essential to survival; they tell us what not to do. As survival needs changed, so did the requirements for happiness. Developing self-awareness helps to eliminate negative feelings.

An element of the Buddhist tradition is a concept known as mindfulness. When we meditate mindfully, we learn to focus without judgment. Mindfulness meditation is the most common type of meditation practiced in the West and perhaps the easiest to begin. It allows happiness to find us.

Gratitude is incredibly powerful if you open your heart to it. Gratitude can improve happiness significantly just by inviting it into your life. It is also a way that you can spread happiness. If you want to be a happy person, you must be grateful.

We showed that self-kindness goes a long way in developing the two key traits that influence your happiness: self-worth and self-esteem. Self-kindness is giving yourself acceptance, patience, caring, and whatever else people use to define kindness. But self-esteem does not determine happiness. While we see that self-esteem may help with happiness, it is not the entire answer. You need to reduce your self-criticism to help boost your self-esteem. By eliminating self-criticism, you can treat yourself with kindness—one pathway to happiness.

Having a strong sense of purpose provides you with a positive, powerful effect. Armed with a sense of purpose, you can leap out of bed each morning, anticipating what is ahead for you in the day. Individuals who can define their "why" can explain their motivation and purpose. Your "why" is essential for several reasons beyond providing your drive and ambition. Your "why" allows you to understand what you are doing in life. *Ikigai* is a process of balancing one's spiritual and practical life for an enjoyable lifestyle while still being productive.

Research has shown how our interactions with family and friends are the key to greater happiness. Our nervous systems expect to have others around us. Studies in biology, neuroscience, and psychology have shown that our bodies operate more efficiently when we are not alone. Friendships are the golden opportunity to build on your happiness power. A study found that individuals who have a secure connection to their community are the happiest.

Numerous research studies have concluded that giving increases happiness in a much more beneficial way than receiving. Charitable giving creates a brain response that imitates those activated by drugs and other stimuli. A German study provided ample evidence that "givers" of time and material things experience greater satisfaction than those who do not. There are many ways to increase your happiness power. To maintain your happiness power, make sure that you do not overextend your giving. You do not want to give so much that you regret what you have done.

Pursuing happiness is a primal instinct. It is an underlying motivator: the pursuit of physical pleasure, our desire to avoid pain, our need for emotional pleasure, and our desire to avoid emotional pain. The more we strive to be happy, the less happy we become. Instead, we become depressed. Your find happiness indirectly. To do so, work on building the five character strengths. If you are too focused on chasing happiness, you might end up chasing it away.

By following this guidance, you can experience all the benefits of the powers of happiness. You will lead a life of fulfillment and well-being. Move slowly, taking actions that are more inherently positive. Over time, you will succeed. You can do it!

As you close this book, remember to smile—it will bolster your happiness quotient. As you return the book to its place on your shelf, remember to take it down and peruse it often. It will continue to reinforce the happiness you so deserve. Thank you for spending time with me. I hope that it has shown you how to be a happier person.

APPENDIX

Words that Express Happiness

You can use these words to describe yourself with an inner dialogue when you encounter negative experiences. Repeat the phrases you compose at least three times. Change them up by selecting different words.

accepted
acclaimed
accomplish
achievement
action
active
admire
adorable
adventure
affirmative
affluent
agree
agreeable
amazing
angelic
beaming
beautiful
believe
beneficial
bliss
bountiful
bounty
brave
bravo
brilliant
bubbly
calm
celebrated

champion
charming
cheery
choice
classic
classical
clean
commend
composed
congratulation
constant
cool
creative
dazzling
delight
delightful
distinguished
divine
ecstatic
effective
effervescent
efficient
effortless
electrifying
elegant
enchanting
encouraging
endorsed

energized
engaging
enthusiastic
essential
esteemed
ethical
excellent
exciting
exquisite
fabulous
fair
familiar
famous
fantastic
favorable
fetching
fine
fitting
flourishing
fortunate
free
fresh
friendly
fun
funny
generous
genius

fortunate
free
fresh
friendly
fun
funny
generous
genius
genuine
giving
glamorous
glowing
good
gorgeous
graceful
great
green
grin
growing
handsome
happy
harmonious
healing
healthy
hearty
heavenly
honest
honorable
honored
hug
idea
ideal
imaginative
imagine
impressive
independent
innovate
innovative
instant
instantaneous
instinctive
intellectual
intelligent
intuitive

inventive
jovial
joy
jubilant
laugh
learned
legendary
light
lovely
lucid
lucky
luminous
outrageous
paradise
perfect
phenomenal
pleasant
pleasurable
plentiful
poised
polished
popular
positive
powerful
prepared
pretty
principled
productive
progress
prominent
protected
proud
safe
satisfactory
secure
seemly
simple
skilled
skillful
smile
soulful
sparkling
special
spirited
spiritual

stirring
stunning
stupendous
success
successful
sunny
super
superb
supporting
surprising
welcome
well
whole
wholesome
willing
wonderful
wondrous
worthy
wow

BIBLIOGRAPHY

1) Sharot, Tali. *The Optimism Bias: A Tour of the Irrationally Positive Brain*. New York: Vintage Books, 2012.

2) Harrar, Sari. "Finding Happiness During Challenging Times." June 16, 2020. https://www.aarp.org/health/healthy-living/info-2020/finding-happiness-during-tough-times.html.

3) Sirios, Maria. *A Short Course in Happiness After Loss*. Housatonic, MA: Green Fire Press. https://artdary.net/pdf/a-short-course-in-happiness-after-loss/

4) BBC News. "Elderly US Woman Lands Plane After Pilot-Husband Dies." April 4, 2012. https://www.bbc.co.uk/news/av/world-us-canada-17606721.

5) Frankl, Victor E. "Those Who Have a 'Why' to Live, Can Bear With Almost Any 'How.'" Accessed month day, year. http://www.knowyourquotes.com/Those-Who-Have-A-Why-To-Live-Can-Bear-With-Almost-Any-How-Viktor-E-Frankl.html.

6) Naya Clinics. "Mindfulness: What Is It and How Can You Do It?" April 23, 2020. https://www.nayaclinics.com/post/mindfulness-what-is-it-and-how-can-you-do-it-1.

7) Tamata, Preeti and Manoj Kumar Rao. "Self-Esteem and Locus of Control among College Students." *Indian Journal of Positive Psychology* 8, no. 2 (2017): 154.

8) Oppong, Thomas. "*Ikigai*: The Japanese Secret to a Long and Happy Life Might Just Help You Live a More Fulfilling." January 10, 2018. https://medium.com/thrive-global/ikigai-the-japanese-secret-to-a-long-and-happy-life-might-just-help-you-live-a-more-fulfilling-9871d01992b7.

9) DiGiulio, Sarah. "In Good Company: Why We Need Other People to Be Happy." January 9, 2018. https://www.nbcnews.com/better/health/good-company-why-we-need-other-people-be-happy-ncna836106.

10) Oppong, Thomas. "Good Social Relationships Are the Most Consistent Predictor of a Happy Life." July 7, 2020. https://goodmenproject.com/featured-content/good-social-relationships-are-the-most-consistent-predictor-of-a-happy-life/.

11) Veny, Mark. "The Link Between Giving and Happiness." January 26, 2018. https://www.healthcentral.com/article/the-link-between-giving-and-happiness.

12) Macmillan, Amanda. "Happiness: Being Generous Makes You Feel Better." July 14, 2017. https://time.com/4857777/generosity-happiness-brain/.

13) Ibid.

14) Ibid.

ABOUT THE AUTHOR

Robert Gill, Jr., a researcher, author, publisher, and businessperson, is best known for the *ArtMolds Journal,* a monthly glossy magazine on art and sculpture that he first published for four years. Robert's previous book, *90 Days to Your First Real Estate Investment Purchase,* is a guide to assist beginners with little money to invest in rental properties. It is based on his forty-plus years of real estate investing. He has written non-fiction books and articles on subjects ranging from teaching, crafts, hobbies, self-help, and cooking to personal finance. He is an avid sailor and lives in Far Hills, New Jersey, with his wife and dog, Ginger.

Robert Gill, Jr., writes and publishes non-fiction books on subjects as far-reaching as personal finance to self-help books. He spends many hours researching the most recent academic studies and revelations on the subjects he writes about. He enjoys Danish and has the body to prove it. His eclectic hobbies include antique car restoration and building projects.

Join those who have signed up for my free happiness newsletter at RobertGillJr.com and get your free copy of *Happiness Secrets*, featuring the latest research for you to improve your happiness. This book is an updated supplement to *Happiness Power*.

With "Happiness Secrets," You're Going to Get . . .

✔ 37 Ways to Boost Your Happiness Immediately
✔ 7 Secrets to Assure Your Happiness and a Maintain Joyful Life
✔ Includes a Happiness and Gratitude Journal to Monitor Your Progress
✔ 20-pages, illustrated, full color for your reading pleasure

➢ <u>Click here: I want your free book</u>

Customer Reviews

⭐⭐⭐⭐⭐ 20

20 customer ratings

5 star		100%
4 star		0%
3 star		0%
2 star		0%
1 star		0%

Share your thoughts with other customers.

All reviewers ⌄

See all customer reviews ›

I would be incredibly thankful if you could take 60 seconds to write a brief review on Amazon, even if it's just a few sentences! Thank you -- Robert

>>Click here to leave a quick review